The Game of
Basketball

*Basketball Fundamentals, and Intangibles
and the Finer Points of the Game
for Coaches, Players, and Fans*

Kevin Sivils

A Southern Family Publishing
KCS Basketball Enterprises, LLC, Katy, Texas

The Game of Basketball:
Basketball Fundamentals, Intangibles
and Finer Points of the Game
for Coaches, Players and Fans

Copyright 2012 Kevin Sivils. All rights reserved.
ISBN: 0615345263
ISBN-13: 9780615345260
Cover design by: Deana Riddle

Published by A Southern Family Publishing
A division of KCS Basketball Enterprises, LLC
www.kcsbasketball.com

"There has never been a book for coaches, players, and fans like *The Game of Basketball*. For the coach this book is about moving a player's game to a higher level. For the player the information in this book can make the difference between being average and good or even great. For the fan who wants to appreciate the sport and the nuances of the game, this book provides many tiny details the average fan is never aware of."

—Rusty Rogers, two-time NAIA Div. II
National Championship coach and two-time
National NAIA Coach of the Year
G37

"This is the stuff that separates the outstanding players from the rest."

—Bill Reidy, veteran high school coach
and skill development instructor

"Once again Kevin Sivils has produced a book that ought to be in every coach's library. Too often we fall into the trap of thinking that Xs and Os are the holy grail, but Coach Sivils reminds us of the truth articulated by John Wooden more than fifty years ago: 'It's not what you do, it's how well you do it.' I've never seen a better compilation of the little things that can turn a basketball player into a Player."

—Doug Porter, head coach, Olivet Nazarene
University Women's Basketball,
eight-time coach of the year

"If you are looking to polish your knowledge of basketball fundamentals, improve your game-management tactics, and fine tune your skills then this book is for you. Coach Sivils does an excellent job of providing a lot of bang for your buck."

—Scott Peterman, college assistant coach

"Coach Sivils writes an instructive and direct guide that covers aspects of the game important to both players and coaches... and a team's success."

—Sarah Ott, varsity center

"Anyone reading this will soon realize that Sivils' advice regarding character (Chapter 10: Character Counts) applies beyond the basketball court to all aspects of a basketball player's life."

—Dr. Yvette Perry, professional educator and sports fan

"When it comes to player development, there is nothing more important than the development of the coach's knowledge of fundamentals and details. Kevin Sivils provides expert advice for coaches desiring to develop that essential base of knowledge."

—Jeremy Donalson, high school coach

"Coach Sivils's advice to ask for input from players has been very helpful... It has created an environment where my players are more focused and pay better attention, allowing me to communicate more effectively."

—Mike Kinslow, middle school coach

"*The Game of Basketball* by Coach Kevin Sivils is a remarkable window into the world's greatest team sport. It's a must read for coaches, players, and fans who want to improve their understanding of the game. The post play chapter is great!"

—Lauren Hall, varsity post player

"I learned things about passing the basketball and running the fast break that really helped me as a point guard."

—Adam Joleson, varsity point guard

"This book addresses nearly every aspect of the game, allowing readers not only to learn effective ways to execute backdoor cutting, high-low passing, or 'box-in' rebounding (to name a few) but also to gain understanding about why [these techniques] work. [The book is] easy to understand and perfect for players wanting to expand and refine their skills."

—Lindsay Quandt, varsity player

"I had no idea the amount of detail that basketball players have to master! I now understand it is not a sport like football or baseball, where a player masters a single position. In basketball a player has to have a complete set of skills even though there are different positions. I enjoy watching the sport so much more now that I have a better appreciation of the finer points of the game."

—Virginia Watts, sports fan and
parent of basketball players

"The chapter on controlling what you can control was insightful for me as a parent in helping my son deal with the inevitable challenges that crop up in a season or a game. I know the skills my son learned in this regard will help him as an adult."

—Sandra Baker, parent of basketball player

"I played football, not basketball, in high school but I always loved the sport as a fan. I watch college basketball games now with a greater appreciation of the really skilled players than I did before."

—Carson Jones, basketball fan

"I wish this book had been available when I started coaching years ago. The reference section alone would have been worth getting the book."

—James Rodgers, high school coach

"This book is filled with practical tips and insights for the novice or experienced coach. This book is straight to the point. The tips and insights from each chapter will save me seasons of trial and error."

—John DiSchiano, high school coach

The Game of
Basketball

*Basketball Fundamentals, and Intangibles
and the Finer Points of the Game
for Coaches, Players, and Fans*

Kevin Sivils

This book is dedicated to my three children, Danny, Katie, and Emily—three blessings from God whom Lisa and I love dearly!

Also by Kevin Sivils:

Game Strategy and Tactics for Basketball: Bench Coaching for Success

Fine Tuning Your Three-Point Attack

Fine Tuning Your Fast Break

Fine Tuning Your Zone Attack Offense

Finding Good Help: Developing and Utilizing Student Assistant Coaches

Better Basketball Practices

Defending the Three-Point Shot

Rebounding: The Game Within the Game

Contents

Acknowledgments

This book is really the result of the efforts of a lot of people, and at the time of its writing most of them were unaware of their contributions. Namely, the content of this book is what these other individuals, all of them coaches or players, contributed. Over the course of my careers as both a player and a coach, I was fortunate to have come in contact with many individuals who shared their basketball knowledge with me. This book is the result of those individuals sharing their wisdom and expertise with me. If I deserve any credit, it is due to the effort I made to learn all of this information about the great game of basketball and teach it to my own players over the course of my coaching career.

It is my hope, like so many of the individuals I have learned from, that by writing this book and sharing this information somehow I will make a tiny contribution for the good of the game I have been fortunate to have been a part of for so many years.

I am sure when I name the coaches and players who helped me so much I will inadvertently leave someone out, but it would be wrong not to name the individuals who imparted their knowledge to me. I first want to acknowledge my college coach, Jack Trager. He always had the time to listen and guide me; he also had the courage to tell me when he did not know the answers to my questions and then steer me to the coach who did. Often that individual was my mentor, the legendary Coach Don Meyer, who at the time of the writing of this book was the winningest coach in the history of NCAA men's basketball.

Other great coaches include Mike Roller, the great post play coach associated with Lipscomb University and Lipscomb High School; Dick Bennett, the great coach from Wisconsin; Rusty Rogers at Houston Christian High School; Bill Reidy, my longtime friend and former assistant coach; and Mark Landry, assistant coach extraordinaire who taught me so much, though I doubt he knows it, about patience and having a servant's heart.

I also want to mention and thank some of my other former assistants and players who helped me learn more about coaching and the game of basketball. My son, Danny, was a great student assistant and former players turned coaches Sam Coates, Robby White, and Michelle Middlebrook. Thanks to players David Coates, who taught me much of what I know about offensive perimeter and point guard play, and Michael Golda, William Looney, and Mike Palmer, who taught me the true meaning of toughness.

Of all the people I wish to acknowledge, I owe the most in my coaching career to my wife, Lisa—one of the best coach's wives ever to bear the title, and my children, who not only supported my coaching career but enjoyed being part of an athletic family.

The Use of Masculine Pronouns in This Book

Masculine pronouns are used throughout this book in an effort to make the language clear by avoiding the cumbersome use of "he or she," "himself or herself," and so on. The use of the masculine pronoun is done in a generic sense. In no way is it meant to be construed as exclusionary, as there are obviously many fine female basketball players, coaches, and fans.

Using This Book

This book is not a source of X's and O's for those seeking to learn more about a particular offense or defense. It does not advocate a particular style or tempo of playing the game of basketball.

It is a source of information about the little details of the game that often are overlooked or untaught. For coaches, players, and fans, this book will give some idea of the finer points of the game. Taking the information in this book and using it can take a team or a player to a higher level.

The book is organized in chapters. The information in each chapter is associated with the primary topic. For example if you're interested in learning more about cutting, you should start with *Chapter Three: The Fine Art of Cutting*. Within each chapter are subheadings that give quick descriptions of the information provided in the following subsections.

Chapter One

Passing and Receiving

Pass Away From the Defense

Many players are skilled at passing technique, but make many bad passes during a game. The resulting turnovers are frustrating to both the player and the coach. The player is frustrated because he used good technique but it resulted in a turnover. The coach is frustrated because the player seemingly passed the ball right to the defender.

The coach might be more at fault than the passer. How can this be true? If the coach has not taught the passer to pass away from the defender, he must shoulder some of the blame.

The concept is simple. The receiver should offer a hand target indicating the direction he will cut to in order to create space between himself and the defender. The passer should pass the ball toward that space, not toward the intended receiver. The receiver should then move to meet the pass, in effect shortening it by shortening the distance between the passer and the receiver.

This concept alone, when players consistently utilize it, will dramatically reduce turnovers and lead to improved execution and greater offensive efficiency.

The Hockey Assist

Hockey may have it right with this concept. In basketball the player who makes the pass that leads to a score, under certain conditions, is awarded an assist. Statisticians in hockey award the last *two* players to touch the puck an assist when the shooter scores a goal!

Players are taught to make the pass that leads to a score. Coaches claim to teach players to make the extra pass. Yet the manner in which players are evaluated for this skill places no weight on the pass leading to the pass that produces the score! Players are going to do what coaches emphasize, not what coaches teach. By recognizing only the player who made the final pass, coaches never statistically reward the player who recognized the play as a good shot developing and passed the ball to the player in position to make the assist pass.

Coaches should consider making another statistical category for evaluating players: the hockey assist. Doing so would recognize players who see plays developing and move the ball to the correct player and court location so a score can be produced on the next pass. Keeping statistics on the hockey assist pass would place an emphasis on this skill. The simple act of measuring it communicates strongly to players this is a valued skill and important to individual and team success, thereby increasing the likelihood players will look to make the extra pass for the best shot possible.

See the Second Defender

Often it is not the obvious defender who makes the steal or intercepts the pass but the second defender who has anticipated the pass. It is easy to recognize the denial defender or the defender the cutter has beaten to get open. It is not as easy to see the help side defender who is anticipating the pass into the low post or to the backdoor cutter cutting to the basket.

The great passers are not the players who see the obvious open passes but the players who can see the second defender who is anticipating the pass in the hope of intercepting it. Coaches can help players develop this skill by adding an extra defender to one-on-one drills and two-on-two drills where part of the drill requires a pass to a cutter who is defended. This simple modification provides an opportunity for the passer to learn to recognize the presence of the second defender and to practice help positioning, anticipating a pass, and intercepting it.

Look Under the Net

The objective of offensive basketball is to score. It is that simple. Players miss many easy scoring opportunities simply because they never see the open players or the easy scoring opportunities.

Players often focus on running the offense or avoiding the defensive pressure instead of looking for easy scoring opportunities. This is not to say the ball handler does not need to focus on running the offense or recognizing defensive pressure. Rather each offensive player must learn to look instinctively for the easy scoring opportunity each time he catches the ball.

This simple but not always easy concept can be instilled by requiring the player in possession of the ball to look under the net before doing anything else on offense. Looking under the net allows the offensive player to see his teammates as well as the defenders. By focusing attention on the area under the net, the ball handler focuses on the most important area of the court: the basket.

Training players to focus on the basket area first and other things second will teach them to see what is going on. The defense may be moving forward to set a trap, but in doing so have left a player under the goal open for an unguarded layup. By seeing everything from the basket area out, the ball handler recognizes where the defenders are and what easy scoring opportunities are available. Looking under the net is a skill that separates great passers from good ones. Players who have developed this skill will be able to see the game much better than those who have not.

Catch the Ball With Your Eyes

Coaches tell players to keep their eyes on the ball, and with good reason. Many mishandled passes are results of players taking their eyes off the ball before catching it.

Telling a player to catch the ball with his eyes is a better concept. It tells the player exactly how long his vision must remain on the ball and aids him in concentrating completely on the ball until it has been caught—in other words all the way into the player's hands. This makes "catch the ball with your eyes" an excellent coaching prompt to improve receiving and catching a pass either when wide open or in defensive traffic.

Turn and Look Up the Court

Finding the opportunity to make an easy pass for a score is often a matter of learning to look. The simplest way for a player to develop this skill is to make a habit of always turning toward the middle of the court, thus allowing himself to see the greatest percentage of the court, and then looking up court.

The second half of this habit is to look under the net. Players should always turn aggressively toward the middle of the court in a triple threat stance and be ready to pass, drive to improve a passing lane or angle, or drive to advance the ball to a more advantageous position on the court.

Fake a Pass to Make a Pass

Moving the defense in order to create an open passing lane, relieve ball pressure on the passer, or move a denial defender away from the receiver is often a necessary tactic, particularly against aggressive pressure, man-to-man defense, or an aggressive zone defense.

The anticipation required to play an aggressive pressure defense in an active zone makes the defense vulnerable to pass fakes. With this in mind, the passer should always use fakes to set up easier passes. The fakes could be away from the intended direction of the pass, toward the intended direction of the pass, or shot fakes to freeze the defense.

The fakes should be short, precise, and sold with enthusiasm. The fakes should not be long, exaggerated, and cause the passer to move the ball outside the center body mass, which could make him lose his balance.

Have Your Legs Ready to Shoot

All too often a player makes a pass that should lead to an easy shot. Yet because the receiver of the pass is not ready to shoot, the defense has enough time to recover and apply enough pressure on the ball to prevent an easy shot.

For the easy shot actually to be taken, both the player in possession of the ball and the potential shooter must recognize a shot opportunity is available. The potential shooter must have his feet properly aligned for the shot, with his knees bent and his hands ready to receive the pass directly in the shooting pocket.

By catching the ball in a shooting stance, the shooter is ready to take the shot upon receiving the ball. Doing all the preparatory work prior to catching the pass allows the shooter to have more time to take a good shot without being hurried by an attacking defender recovering to the ball.

Veer Away From the Cutter

Creating a passing lane for a pass that leads to an easy score is an excellent tactic for a ball handler leading a fast break attack. The most common defense to slow an attacking fast break is the two defender tandem: one defender sprints back to defend the rim until a second defender can sprint past, allowing the first defender to attack the ball aggressively in an effort to disrupt the fast break.

This strategy utilizes a tandem alignment, with the first defender attempting to stop the ball in the area of the three-point line in the center of the floor. The second defender takes the first pass to either the left or right side while the first defender sprints back to cover the rim and defend against the across-the-lane pass.

The goal of this strategy is to prevent a quick one-pass shot resulting in an easy score. If the defense is able to force two passes and not allow a shot, the other three defenders should arrive in time to force the attacking offensive players to pull the ball out and set up their half-court offense.

In order to overcome this tactic, the smart offensive player will suddenly veer away from the player who is the best finisher filling one of the lanes on the fast break, be it a two-player or three-player attack. By veering away from the intended receiver and putting the ball into the hand on the side of the intended receiver, the ball handler can create an open passing lane.

This tactic will cause the first defender to attack the ball in an effort to stop the penetrating dribble toward the goal. By veering to one side, the second defender, who must cover the first pass, will shift to the same side of the court the ball handler is veering toward in anticipation of a pass toward that side. By doing so both defenders create an open pass for an easy scoring opportunity for the best finisher.

By changing the ball to the hand on the side of the best finisher, if possible, the ball handler eliminates the need to bring the ball across his body in front of the on the ball defender in order to make the pass.

Follow the First Pass on the Break

Aggressive defensive teams spend lots of time developing their abilities to make defensive transitions with great speed. Often these teams are trained, and with good reason, to defend the area around the rim first and then establish their defensive schemes from the rim out.

As a result of this tactic, good defensive teams will try to force one pass, then stop the receiver from shooting or penetrating after receiving the pass. This one or two seconds of delay buys the aggressive defensive team the time it needs for its other defenders to sprint to the area around the rim and then begin to establish the defense from the rim out.

Even against solid defensive teams such as the one described, it is still possible to obtain an excellent shot quickly by simply having the player who leads the fast break follow his pass to the elbow of the lane on the side of the court to which the ball is passed. If the defense is able to stop the initial attack and get its defenders back to the rim, this simple maneuver will leave the passer open for a high-percentage fifteen-foot jump shot. If the passer is an outstanding three-point shooter, he should spot up for a three-on-the-lane line extended on the side of the court to which the ball is passed.

Shorten the Pass by Stepping To It

For decades coaches have told players to meet passes in an effort to encourage offensive players to pursue passes and catches aggressively, thus preventing aggressive defenders from intercepting the pass. This might not be the best direction to give players in order to achieve the desired result.

A better approach is for players to shorten the pass by stepping to the ball when it is passed. While the two commands are intended to produce the same result, for an offensive player who can catch a pass in traffic or under heavy denial pressure almost every time, the two commands are not equally effective. Perhaps players can visualize the concept of a shorter pass better than the concept of meeting the pass.

Another variable might be the command to step toward the ball while it is in flight. This is more detailed and specific than meeting the pass.

Regardless of why it works, coaches would be wise to adopt this verbal cue, and players would be equally wise to make this simple intangible a part of their game.

Use a Drop Pass

Catching the ball in traffic is a different and often more difficult task for post players than for other players. The post player is not only surrounded by a number of defensive players attempting to deflect the entry pass but also must hold a seal to maintain position against a defensive player determined to move the post player out of the desired position and location.

To make it easier for the post player to catch the ball, when an offensive player is able to drive and penetrate the lane, drawing a defender from a post player and creating a passing opportunity, a drop bounce pass should be used. This affords the post player the best chance to catch the ball successfully.

A regular bounce pass or a chest pass will have too much velocity, making the ball more difficult for the post player to handle. A drop pass is easier to handle and often allows the passer to be more accurate in placing the pass between a number of defenders.

Making the Backdoor Pass

From an artistic standpoint, there are few plays in the game of basketball more pleasing to the eye than a perfectly executed backdoor play. On the surface this is a simple play, which is perhaps why it's so appealing to fans when perfectly executed.

However if this play is so easy, why do so many teams play pressure defenses, which are vulnerable to the backdoor pass? The answer is also simple: the backdoor pass and cut is not as easy to execute as it seems. Executing the backdoor cut is addressed in the chapter on cutting, but this point needs to be made clear so you will understand the manner in which the backdoor pass must be made. It's not enough to beat the defender backdoor; the cutter must be able to receive the ball and score. Herein lies the problem.

Most backdoor passes do indeed beat the defenders, but the pass is not thrown in a way the cutter can receive the ball or do something positive after receiving it. The main issue is space—having room both to catch the ball and then to make a pass or score a basket. Most passers pass the ball at a bad angle, thus failing to create the needed space for the cutter.

The type of pass used can also be problematic. Direct chest or overhead passes can be difficult for the cutter to catch due to the velocity of the ball and the angle of the pass.

The solution to both problems is to pass the ball only in a manner that provides the needed space and ensures the cutter can catch the ball. To make a successful backdoor pass every time, the passer needs only to pass the ball directly down the lane line, perpendicular to the baseline, using a bounce pass. If necessary he should drive to the lane line extended to make the pass.

By using this technique, the cutter will obtain possession of the ball just outside of the lane, ensuring sufficient space is available to catch and shoot the ball. The bounce pass, while quick, lessens the velocity of the ball sufficiently so the cutter can successfully handle it.

This concept is simple to demonstrate and easy for players to learn. Adding this to a player's repertoire will make him a much better passer. If you can see the post player's number the ball must be passed into the post.

Few things frustrate a post player as much as working hard to obtain position and having a perimeter player simply take one look inside, or worse yet no look at all, and then reverse the ball. Even teams who rely on the three-point shot as their primary offensive weapon stress the importance of inside scoring and its direct relationship to winning basketball games.

Granted these teams' approaches can be deceiving. They also rely on offensive rebounds for one fourth to one third of their points and on penetration to create the three-point opportunities. While it's true these teams' post players may not score a lot of traditional back-to-the-basket goals, they shoot higher-than-normal field goal percentages for their positions, and when open the ball goes inside to them.

Given that teams that do not rely on traditional post plays make efforts to get the ball to their post players, why is it that teams that play a traditional half-court style sometimes do not enter the ball into the low post? This tactic yields the needed high-percentage two-point field goals and creates opportunities to draw fouls.

It's simple actually. The perimeter players have not internalized this rule. When they can see the post player's numbers on his chest, the ball must be entered into the post, though the post player does not have to shoot.

The simple act of passing the ball into the post creates a long list of problems for the defense, as the offensive low post is an excellent place both to score from and to pass from. The ball's being in the low post also requires some type of defensive reaction if the offensive post player is any threat at all, thus creating scoring opportunities for other players.

This rule applies to players who are not traditional back-to-the-basket post players as well. A guard who has cut into the low post area and is showing his numbers should receive the ball.

Catch the Ball With Feet in the Air

This skill is part of shortening the pass and has several advantages. A player who catches the ball with his feet in the air can quick stop or jump stop and avoid establishing a pivot foot by having both feet contacting the court at the same time.

The second half of this skill is to land facing the basket in a triple threat stance—ready to shoot, pass, or drive. To do this the player must jump off the inside foot and turn into the pass. He can eliminate any forward or sideways momentum by dropping his behind two inches and then rising up two inches.

By adopting this skill players are ready to attack upon receiving the ball. They have the additional advantage of not having established a pivot foot, allowing them to attack with either foot. This skill, when combined with shortening the pass, will allow a player to reduce turnovers dramatically.

Feeding the Post

Every basketball player must master the skill of feeding the post. There are only four ways a single post defender can defend a post player: high side denial, baseline denial, behind, or with a dead front. Each of these tactics has its strong points, and often the defense's total scheme determines which tactic you should use.

Like anything else, each of these tactics has weaknesses as well. Knowing them allows the post player and the passer to work together to enter the ball into the post, hopefully for a scoring attempt.

The first concept the passer needs to be aware of is the pass is the key that allows the post player to react and shoot, eliminating the need to think, denying the defense the split second it needs to recover and successfully defend against a shot. The passer, when looking to feed the post, must always think, *Pass to score*.

The second concept the passer must use is the idea of passing away from the defense. Combine these two concepts with accurate passing and the offense now has a significant advantage.

When the defender is denying the post from the high side, the ball must be passed or dribbled to a location on the floor below the low post offensive player. This will allow a pass to be made to the baseline side of the offensive post player. Utilizing a bounce pass with some English, or spin, allows the ball to be thrown even farther away from the post defender, yet the ball will bounce back to the offensive post player. This type of pass on the baseline side tells the offensive post player a simple catch and score shot, or drop step, is available on the baseline side. The post player can then focus on receiving the ball, chinning it, and executing the post move for a score.

If the post defender is denying on the baseline side or changes position to the baseline side, the pass is keyed to the middle. A crisp flick or chest pass is made away from the baseline defender. The offensive post player knows a pass away from the baseline means he'll have a shot attempt by turning to the middle of the lane.

Playing directly behind a low post offensive player may seem like an unwise tactic—like simply allowing the ball to be entered with ease into the offensive low post. If the offensive post player is not a particularly strong scoring threat but an excellent offensive rebounder, this is an excellent tactic, allowing the defender to prevent the offensive low post from obtaining offensive rebounds by keeping an inside rebounding position at all times.

This tactic is also successful even with an excellent offensive post player if the defense uses a collapsing cover-down strategy with quick perimeter defenders.

The entry pass in this situation must be directly to the offensive post player's numbers. This communicates the defender is directly behind, and the offensive post player must execute a post move to score. The half second gained in this method of communication may be enough to beat the collapsing perimeter defenders and obtain an excellent shot.

Teams that choose to dead front the offensive low post do so for two reasons: to prevent the ball from entering the offensive low post and so the low post defender can help on the ball side of the floor.

As intimidating as this tactic may appear—and it is a good defensive tactic—the ball can be easily entered into the offensive low post by quickly passing it to the top of the key while the offensive low post player seals the low post defender out of the lane.

The passer on the top of the key passes the ball to the corner of the ball side backboard. This forces the offensive low post to move to catch the pass. It also moves the offensive low post player away from the help side defender and low post defender and creates a quick shot opportunity. The pass must be crisp, not a soft lob, and slightly above the head of the offensive low post player.

The least ideal pass to enter the ball into the offensive low post is the lob pass, particularly from the wing. A lob pass is slow and creates several problems including the help side defense positioning to draw a charge from the offensive low post; the offensive low post player pushing off the low post defensive player, which is an offensive foul; and the defense deflecting the pass, creating a turnover.

In order to negate these drawbacks, the offensive low post should seal the low post defender out of the lane and put both arms up above his head. The lob pass should not be directly to the offensive low post player's head but to the corner of the backboard. The offensive low post player should hold his position until the ball is directly overhead and then move to receive it.

This tactic virtually eliminates the offensive charging foul as well as the pushing foul. In addition the location of the pass makes it more difficult for the defense to anticipate the pass, making a successful deflection less likely.

Chapter Two

Defense

Hand Discipline on Defense

Defensive players should only foul for profit so their team can gain an advantage over the opponent. Fouls committed as a result of real and not false hustle—such as attempting to block out, gaining a defensive position in the low post, or diving for a loose ball—are acceptable in almost every game situation. Fouls committed for any other reason are not. The most common reason for negative fouls is a lack of hand discipline.

Make the Offensive Player Put the Ball on the Floor

An offensive player who has the option of passing, shooting, or driving is truly a triple threat. The on-the-ball defender must dictate that two of the three threats be negated.

This is best done by forcing the offensive player to put the ball on the floor. The defender must not allow the offensive player to dribble in a penetrating manner, but rather to the outside of the court.

Dictate the Direction of the Drive

The on-the-ball defender must make every effort to dictate the drive of the offensive player. This will put the ball on the floor and then drive it to the outside area of the court, preferably toward the baseline in the corner.

In addition the on-the-ball defender should encourage, through ball pressure, the offensive player to pick up the dribble, creating a dead situation.

Playing the Dead Call

When an offensive player kills his dribble, the on-the-ball defender should immediately crowd him, creating an uncomfortable environment by violating the offensive player's personal zone.

To create maximum pressure on the ball and increase the possibility of a turnover, as soon as the offensive player kills the dribble, the on-the-ball defender should throw his feet at the offensive player's pivot foot. Crowding the pivot foot will cause the offensive player to lean away from the pressure, and he will not be able to pivot without traveling.

In addition to this tactic, the on-the-ball defender must call "dead" so his teammates are aware the dribble has been killed, allowing the defenders to deny every pass and force a turnover or a five-second count.

High Hands on a Closeout

Defensive coaching legend Dick Bennett believed one of the most important individual defensive techniques was for a defender to have high hands when closing out. Bennett claimed when his teams gave up an unusually high defensive team field goal other four defenders to deny a pass to the offensive player they are responsible for percentage (the opponent shot a higher than usual field goal percentage), he could trace it back to not having high hands when closing out. This allowed the shooters to have a better look at the rim, thereby increasing their success. This technique was so important to Bennett that if a defender did nothing else correctly when close to the player with the ball, that single correctly executed technique was to have high hands.

Think *Shot* but Play Drive

Another coaching legend, Don Meyer, believes when a defender closes out on the ball, the defender must be thinking *shot* (which means high hands) but playing the drive. This means that when the defender breaks down and uses a patter step, or short, choppy steps, to close on the ball, his weight should be on the back foot. This will allow him to reverse direction with a bit more ease and allow a quicker recovery from the offensive player's attacking drive.

Do Not Allow the Shooter to Get a Clean Look at the Shooting Target

One of the keys to being successful on any given shot attempt is for the shooter to have a good view, called a *clean look*, of the rim or square on the backboard. Conversely, in order to create as much difficulty for the shooter as possible, the on-the-ball defender should do everything possible to prevent the shooter from obtaining the desired clean look at the rim. The best method is to have high hands. Simply this is having both hands over the defender's head, with the elbows by the his or her ears, and either with the fingers pointing straight up at the ceiling or with the wrists bent back at a ninety-degree angle.

Waving the hands, swinging wildly to fake a shot block, or lunging at the shooter's feet may distract weaker shooters but will have no impact on a good shooter. These techniques are also very affective on the pump or shot fake, drawing the defender into fouling or giving the offensive player an opportunity to drive and penetrate the defense.

Contesting the shot is a situation wherein the defense must be consistent and play the percentages. High hands to block the shooter's view of the target may not be glamorous, but it gets the job done time after time. The other techniques are best described as false hustle and are attempts by the defender to cover up mistakes in closing out on the ball in time. Players must be consistent with this technique. It will reduce the opponent's field goal percentage and driving opportunities, the total number of fouls committed by the defense, and both individual and team fouls.

Contesting the Shot Is Better Than Blocking the Shot

This technique is a hard sell to most players. A blocked shot is intimidating, but it's exciting to both players and fans even though it's a very low-percentage play.

There are gifted shot blockers who should be allowed to block shots, but note: if you watch them, they are often more interested in contesting or touching shots to deflect them rather than in swatting a shot into the stands. Celtic great Bill Russell, an extremely skilled shot blocker, would occasionally swat a shot into the stands for intimidation purposes, but preferred instead to deflect a shot gently into the hands of a waiting teammate so the Celtics could start their vaunted fast-break attack.

Why is contesting the shot better than attempting to block a shot? An examination of what can happen is a good way to answer this question. If the defender attempts to block a shot and fails to do so, the following usually happens: he commits a foul; he lands in a poor defensive position; and if the shot was faked into a blocked-shot attempt, the shooter will easily beat him with a real shot attempt or a drive. It also always leaves the defender in a poor rebounding position, allowing the shooter to have a nearly unrestricted path to the goal for an offensive rebound attempt.

Contesting the shot allows the defender to deny the shooter a clean look at the rim and prevents unnecessary fouls. Shot blocking, except for individual players who are consistently successful, should not only not be allowed but should be looked upon as hero defense—another example of false hustle to allow a player to deny responsibility for a defensive mistake.

When Contesting a Shot, Be the Second Player to Leave the Ground

Contesting the shot is of major importance in any defensive scheme, and it is vital that the individual defensive player correctly carries it out. It is also important that the defensive player doesn't succumb to a shot fake, thereby fouling or allowing for a penetrating drive by the offensive player.

To build the habits needed to contest the shot every time and not fall prey to the shot fake and other bad habits players can develop defensively when guarding the shooter, the defensive player must build the habit of never leaving the ground before the shooter. This eliminates fouling, attempting to block shots, and leaving the defender vulnerable to penetration after a successful shot fake. Using this approach the defender will still be able to contest the shot successfully and take away the shooter's clean look.

Contact on Defense Will Negate Speed and Quickness

Speed and quickness give the offensive player a tremendous advantage over a slower defensive player. One way to negate this advantage is to make physical contact with the offensive player at every opportunity. This will not only slow him down; it will also frustrate him and disrupt the smooth flow of the offense.

This tactic is not an excuse to play dirty basketball and cheap shot the opponent's star player. Nor is it permission for the defensive player to foul at will. It requires the defensive player to be sharp mentally, execute with flawless technique, and always be on the lookout for an opportunity to create the desired contact.

There are many ways a player can create physical contact without having a foul called. One is beating a cutter to the spot and chesting him up, thus denying him the desired spot on the court. Another is having the second defender bump a cutter as he comes off a screen, slowing the cutter long enough for his defender to recover.

The defender can crowd the offensive player at every feasible opportunity. This tactic is particularly effective if the offensive player has picked up his dribble. The defender must crowd the pivot foot in this instance.

Early Help Is Never a Mistake on Defense

Dick Bennett coined the phrase *early help* as part of his famous push and pack man-to-man defensive systems. Early help is the idea that the help defender can make a mistake by arriving too late to help the on-the-ball defender, yet it will never be a mistake for the help defender to assist the on-the-ball defender before he needs it.

Experience has shown Bennett to be correct in this assessment of help situations. Helping early ensures the help defender is on time, is almost always in the correct position, and decreases the number of needless fouls due to arriving too late to help stop dribble penetration by the offense.

Anticipate the Offense Two Passes Away on Defense

Anticipation is an essential mental skill for all defenders, and even more so for defenders with average or below-average speed. Anticipation allows defenders to act instead of react.

Anticipating two passes away allows the individual defender to plan his move from a help position to a denial position or any variety of defensive situations, such as stopping penetration, blocking out for a rebound, or collapsing on the offensive low post.

Anticipating two passes away also allows the defender to move while the ball is in the air on the first of the two passes and cheat toward the position that will be needed on the second pass. This slight edge is often necessary to prevent the offense from scoring or gaining an advantage that will lead to a scoring opportunity. It may also allow the defense to disrupt the flow of the offense and force a turnover.

Move While the Ball Is in the Air

The individual defensive player and the entire defense as a unit, regardless of the style of defense they play, should move and adapt their positions while the ball is in the air. If the defender and the unit stand while the ball is passed and then adjust their positions after the receiver catches the ball, it will be too late to pressure the offense successfully and prevent the offense from executing as it desires.

The defender and the defensive unit should anticipate the pass and then, once it's made, sprint in the same direction. This ingrained habit will go a long way toward consistently correct defensive positioning when the offense moves the ball by passing.

Sprint While the Ball Is in the Air

"What is the best way to move when changing defensive positions after the offense has passed the ball?" It's an age-old question, and the answer is to sprint in the direction of the ball while it is in the air.

This concept builds the all-important habit of quick, aggressive repositioning that allows the defense to present a hustling and hostile environment for the offense to operate against.

Arrive When the Ball Arrives

Arriving early is always a good idea when playing defense. Arriving too late on defense leads to nothing but problems for the defensive unit.

Defensive players should develop a habit of arriving at the same time the ball does regardless of what player or position they're defending. The advantage of having five defensive players arriving at their designated positions is they will have finished adjusting position when the receiver catches the ball. This negates any momentary advantage gained by passing the ball in combination with cutting and screening. It also allows the new on-the-ball defender to apply immediate and intense pressure on the receiver, disrupting the flow of the offense and potentially forcing a turnover.

Stay Below the Shoulders of the Offensive Player

How low should a defensive stance be in order to be effective? A good rule of thumb is for the defender to attempt to keep the top of his head below the shoulders of the offensive player he's defending. This is an effective and practical means to teaching players to judge the required depths of their stances.

Make the Ball Handler Pick Up the Dribble on a Ball Screen

The pick and roll has long been a staple in the game of basketball, particularly in the NBA. In recent years it has enjoyed a resurgence in college and high school games. It is an effective offensive tactic, forcing the defense to react to a screen and cover a cutter.

One of the best strategies to defend the pick and roll is to force the ball handler to pick up the dribble. This eliminates the threat of dribble penetration, allowing the on-the-ball defender to pressure the ball without fear. The defender of the screener can then focus totally on covering the cut the screener makes, usually to the goal.

There are several methods that can encourage the ball handler to pick up the dribble. The easiest is simply to have both the on-the-ball defender and the screener's defender trap the ball handler. This method requires a third teammate to cover the screener/cutter.

A second method requires the defender of the screener to show help early, possibly faking a trap, to discourage the use of the screen. The object is to encourage the ball handler to believe a trap is coming or that the second defender has committed, leaving the screener open to slip the screen for a pass. For this method to be successful, the second defender must be adept at both faking the trap/showing early help and anticipating the screener's slip screen. If the second defender can take away the pass on the slipped screen, the ball handler has no immediate passing opportunity, and the pick and roll has been defeated.

The third method is the most difficult but the safest. The second defender calls screen to alert the on-the-ball defender to the fact that a pick and roll screen is about to be set. The on-the-ball defender gets into the ball handler by getting as close as possible.

As the screener approaches, the second defender shows early help in an effort to cause the ball handler to hesitate. The on-the-ball defender skinnies up by stepping through and over the screener, using both a leg and an arm to establish position in a gap between the ball handler and the screener. This tactic neutralizes the screen and forces the ball handler to drive in a wider than desired path. Hopefully this will cause the ball handler to pick up the dribble. The second defender then must recover to a denial position as quickly as possible, preventing a pass to the screener/cutter.

Despite the difficulty of this method, it is the safest, as the screener/cutter is always covered and there is no need for a third defensive player to rotate to cover an open cutter.

Drawing a Charge Is the Best Play in Basketball

Drawing a charge is fast becoming a lost art. Some coaches decry teaching it, claiming anyone can draw a charge—it requires no special skill or athletic ability. As far as the latter, this might be true. But in terms of skill, this statement is false. Regardless, it does take some courage to stand still and let another human being run you down.

When a player draws a charge, the opponent loses possession of the ball. If a field goal was scored in the commission of the charge, the points are waived off. A foul is added to the opponent's team foul total *and* the individual foul total of the player who committed the charge. The team of the player who drew the charge is then closer to shooting one and one and is awarded possession of the ball. The player who committed the charge may be hesitant to drive to the goal again out of fear of committing another charging foul.

Drawing a charge is the best play in the game of basketball because it helps a team defend the baseline and lane on middle penetration. It is a valuable tool for team defense. Teams that draw several charges in a game build strong reputations for mental and physical toughness on defense—an important pregame mental edge for any team.

Force the Offensive Player Out of His Sweet Spot

Every basketball player has a favorite spot on the court to shoot from, pass from, or drive from. It's called his *sweet spot*. If the offensive player can occupy his sweet spot, the chance of a positive offensive outcome increases dramatically.

The defense wants to prevent the offensive player from occupying his sweet spot. This doesn't mean keeping the offensive player away from the sweet spot. Usually, simply forcing the player out of the spot by two or three feet is enough to reduce the positive impact of the sweet spot dramatically.

Defensive players can use several different tactics to achieve this. The first is to play tough denial defense, forcing the offensive player to receive the ball several feet from the sweet spot. The second is to crowd the offensive player, forcing him to dribble. Third, by steering the offensive player in the direction desired by the defense, the defensive player will successfully force the offensive player from the sweet spot.

Another excellent tactic is trapping the offensive player when he catches the ball in his sweet spot. When the offensive player catches the ball in his sweet spot, the defense automatically traps the offensive player. This forces the player to leave the sweet spot or pass the ball to a teammate. This tactic requires all five defenders and is the most difficult to perfect.

Chapter Three

The Fine Art of Cutting

Move With a Purpose

Movement without a purpose is not only of no use, it is often counterproductive. Players who have no clear and correct reason to move often disrupt the purposeful and useful movement of other teammates. For example a player cutting with no clear and positive purpose could eliminate another player's opportunity to cut to an open area near the goal for a pass and a layup. The player with no purpose could bring a defensive player into the passing lane or simply clog up the lane area, closing the opening for a potential pass for a score.

Purposeful movement includes cutting to an open area to receive a pass for a shot, continuing moving the ball for a shot, setting a screen for a teammate, creating space for a pass or dribble penetration, or moving the ball up the court. Movement be purposeful not only in terms of location but also in how the cutting movement is made.

Change Direction and Change Pace

The basic type of cut used to get open for a pass is the V-cut. All V-cuts should involve both a change of direction and a change of pace. Change of direction can best be described as going in one direction and then moving at a ninety degree angle. A change of pace means the player will make a dramatic change in speed at the same time he changes direction. In addition the player must change direction with a cut that resembles a precise angle, not a curve.

In Slow and Out Fast When Cutting

Players often make the mistake of not changing speed when executing a V-cut. It's much easier for the defense to react to a constant speed, even when combined with a change in direction, than to a change of direction combined with a change of pace.

When executing a V-cut, the player should enter the cut moving at a slow speed, change direction, then accelerate quickly. Walking is an acceptable form of slowly entering the V-cut.

Standing Still

Standing still is a form of change of pace, particularly when the player is running at full speed. In order for there to be the required change of pace as well as a change of direction, the player must stop and stand still. Standing still and then changing direction forces the defender to guess when the cutter will move, and even with good anticipation the defender will lag behind the cutter, producing the desired space for the cutter to receive a pass.

The Gretzky Rule: Cut to Where the Shot Will Be

Wayne Gretzky has often said he scored so many points in hockey games not because he was a great goal scorer or passer, but because he skated to where the puck would be instead of where the puck was.

This concept applies to basketball as well. Players without the ball should cut to the open area where the shot is. The player with the ball will then be able to move the ball via a pass to where the shot will be. If a player does not cut into the open area for a shot, the ball handler has no opportunity to pass for a score.

You Must Go Somewhere When You Move

This concept is different from the idea of moving with a purpose. Players can desire to get open, enter the v-cut slowly, exit quickly, and use a ninety degree angle and still not be able to get open.

In order for a change of direction to be successful, the player must cover at least fifteen feet in both legs of the cut. In other words the player must go somewhere. By moving the defender fifteen feet in one direction and then combining a change of pace with an angle cut and a change of direction with a fifteen-foot sprint in the new direction, the cutter will make the task of defending him as difficult as possible.

Hands Up When You Come Out of a Cut

The primary purpose of cutting is to get open in order to receive a pass. In order to reduce the possibility of a turnover due to not catching the pass, a player should build the habit of bringing up his hands to provide a target and creating a pocket to catch the ball. By developing this habit, the cutter will seldom mishandle a pass due to not having his hands ready to catch the ball.

Start Steps

Start steps are known by a wide variety of other names, such as *direct drive, crossover step,* and *accelerating from a standing position when cutting.* Start steps are what a player makes when stepping forward to execute a pass. By using the term *start step* to describe the movement, players have less to remember and are more likely to execute the desired movement correctly each time it is required.

Start steps should be long, low, and straight. The player must travel in the direction his big toe on his stepping foot points. This is also the direction the ball will take when a pass is made. Start steps should always be in a direct line toward the goal, the desired cutting area, or the intended target when passing.

Quick stops

Quick stops, also called *jump stops*, are a method players can use to stop quickly at an exact spot. They prevent the offensive player from establishing a predetermined pivot foot when stopping if the player is in possession of the ball.

To execute a quick stop, the player takes what is essentially a start step, executes a low-height jump, brings both feet together underneath his body, reaches out for the court like a bird reaching for a branch when landing, and makes contact with the court with both feet at the same time. The player lands in a triple-threat stance, maintaining excellent body balance.

The key t0 executing a quick stop correctly is for the player to ensure his feet are no higher than two or three inches off the court while airborne and for both feet to contact the court at the same time when he lands, with the entire foot surface making contact.

Jump Catch

A jump catch involves a quick stop at the same time the player catches the ball. This skill allows the player to shorten a pass aggressively by stepping to the ball while it's in flight, executing a quick stop, and, while in the air, reaching out, grabbing, and tucking the ball into the pocket. Finally he lands and stops with both feet contacting the court at the same time in triple-threat position.

The jump catch forces the player to shorten the pass, thereby reducing turnovers, and the player does not establish a pivot foot upon catching the ball. If at all possible, the player should land facing the basket, looking under the net for offensive opportunities.

Triple-Threat Position

This stance is so named because a player can shoot, pass, or drive from it when in possession of the ball. In fact, before a player can execute any of these basic skills, he must be in this stance.

The triple-threat position is essentially the universal athletic stance of feet spread hip width apart with one foot slightly forward, the hips and knees bent to lower the center of gravity, head centered between the feet, and the ball in the shooting pocket.

Players must learn the habit of assuming the triple-threat stance when they have the ball. Every time a player catches the ball or picks up his dribble, he must assume the triple threat position.

Turn and Face/Look Under the Net

Players assuming the triple-threat position after gaining possession of the ball is excellent, but it is only a start. In order for the triple-threat position to be effective, the player must be facing his offensive goal. This allows him to see if a shot, pass, or drive is available. The offensive player must also look under the net. This allows him to see teammates cutting to open areas on the floor, open driving lanes, and the location of all defensive players, particularly those playing help defense.

The Two-Inch Rule

Forward momentum has caused many an offensive player to charge, shoot off balance what could have been a good shot, or shoot a shot long because he drifted too far into it. In order to eliminate forward or another kind of undesired momentum, after stopping quickly the offensive player should drop his buttocks two inches lower than normal and then rise back up to a normal triple-threat position. This short downward movement transfers all of the undesired momentum straight down, allowing the player to stop completely before performing the next skill sequence, be it a jump shot or a pivot.

Chapter Four

Attack Basketball

Go Somewhere With Your Dribble

When a player puts the ball on the floor to dribble, he should have a specific location on the court he intends to move to by dribbling. Too many players dribble simply for the sake of doing it. By putting the ball on the floor just to dribble, the player loses the element of surprise in attacking the defense. Before the offensive player can pass or shoot, he must pick up his dribble, giving the defense a split second to adjust and defend accordingly.

Drive in a Straight Line

The shortest distance between two points is a straight line. The quickest way to travel from point A to point B is by traveling in a straight line.

Players have a tendency to dribble drive in an arc, giving the defense a chance to adjust and recover. In fact defenders who are good on the ball try to force the ball handler to drive in an arc.

However driving in a straight line gives the defense the least amount of time to react and adjust. It increases the likelihood that the offensive player will be able to drive to his desired location on the court successfully, score, complete a pass to an open teammate, and/or draw a foul.

Get From the Three-Point Line to the Rim in One Dribble

An essential skill for the great three-point shooter is to be able to catch a pass and then drive from the three-point line to the goal in one dribble. An essential skill for the great penetrator is to be able to catch a pass and drive from the three-point line to the goal in one dribble.

Driving to the rim in one dribble forces the player to attack aggressively, drive in a straight line, and use the fewest dribbles possible, and gives the defense the least amount of time to react and adjust.

Players as young as sixth grade can learn this skill, which creates the ability to explode to the rim quickly. For the great outside shooter, the ability to attack the rim in a single dribble prevents the defender from closing out quickly and crowding the shooter, creating an opportunity for the shooter to explode to the rim and score. By obtaining space through the threat of the explosive drive, the shooter purchases some additional time to get a good outside shot off.

The great penetrator must be able to get to the rim in one dribble. This creates a sense of heightened awareness on the part of the defense. When the penetrator attacks, the defense will aggressively give help in an effort to stop the him. In doing so the defense will create passing lanes of opportunity for the penetrator, allowing him to pass to a teammate for an easy scoring opportunity.

Dribble With a Purpose or Not at All

Players too often catch the basketball and immediately begin to dribble. Doing so eliminates two of the three threats of the triple-threat position. When a player has the use of the dribble and is in triple-threat position, he can shoot, pass, or drive. By dribbling, the player has eliminated two of the three threats without any pressure from the defense.

Good defensive teams work very hard to pressure the offensive player with the ball to put it on the floor and then dribble it to an undesirable offensive location. The offensive player should only dribble when he has a clear purpose and destination in mind and when dribbling is the only way the ball can be moved to that location.

Dribble the Ball Only to Score, Improve a Passing Angle, or Advance the Ball up the Court

There are only three reasons to dribble a basketball: to drive it for a scoring opportunity, to improve a passing angle to a teammate, and to advance the ball up the court if it cannot be advanced by passing it.

Use a Pull-Back Crossover Dribble Move to Beat a Trap

When faced with an impending defensive trap, the ball handler should select one of the two defenders to beat and then use a dribble move known as a *pull-back crossover* to defeat the trap. In this technique the ball handler power dribbles twice toward the approaching trapping defenders to encourage them to attack. The ball handler then executes two power back dribbles to draw the trapping defenders toward the ball.

The ball handler now has one of two options. (In this example he is dribbling the ball in his right hand to initiate the pull-back crossover.) The first is to execute a 180-degree rear pivot while also executing a low, tight crossover dribble from the right to left hand and stepping in front of the ball with the right leg to protect it from the approaching defenders. The ball handler then accelerates to beat the defender on the left side of the trap.

The second option, after executing the two power back dribbles, would be to accelerate forward without using the crossover move, keeping the ball in the same hand. This tactic uses the forward momentum of the right defender against the defender.

In both examples the ball handler did not beat both defenders on the dribble, but instead isolated the weaker of the two defenders and then attacked the trap.

Always Aggressively Turn and Face the Basket in a Triple-Threat Stance

Regardless of where the offensive player takes possession of the ball, by either receiving a pass or grabbing a rebound or a loose ball, the first move he must always make is to aggressively turn and face his offensive basket. Then he can establish a good triple-threat position.

This tactic prevents many unnecessary turnovers, charging fouls, or steals. It also sets an aggressive mental approach to always attack or look for ways to attack as soon as the player transitions from defense to offense.

Look Under the Net After Facing Up in Triple Threat

After aggressively facing the basket in triple threat, the first action the offensive player must take is to look under his offensive net. This skill allows the player to survey the court and view the location of the offensive and defensive players. It also allows the offensive player to recognize quickly what opportunities exist to pass, drive, or initiate the offense based on where the defenders are. This single habit can increase the number of easy baskets scored in a game by four to six, simply by recognizing the opportunities available.

Four Dribbles Is All You Need to Push the Ball up the Court

Ball handlers should always be as efficient as possible with the dribble. Just as the ball handler should drive from the three-point line to the rim in one dribble, the ball handler should advance the ball up the court with the fewest number of dribbles possible.

An aggressive ball handler running at maximum speed can advance the ball up the court in four dribbles. Players who are not able to do this should work to develop this skill. Ball handlers who can advance the ball with just four dribbles are extremely difficult for the defense to stop on the open floor. Not only is the minimalist approach difficult to defend, but it creates numerous scoring and passing opportunities.

The Last Dribble Must Be Difficult

The last dribble a ball handler takes should be a bit harder than normal. This makes it easier for him to pick the dribble up quickly and aggressively and chin it for a layup or to quickly snap it to the chest in order to pass the ball. A final hard dribble also allows the ball handler to get the ball to the shooting pocket quicker, allowing a quicker shot to be taken off the dribble without the shooter's having to worry.

Sweep the Ball to Create Space

Excellent on-the-ball defenders will crowd an offensive player as soon as he receives a pass or grabs a rebound or loose ball. In order to create space to maneuver, pass, or shoot, the offensive player should aggressively face up to the offensive basket while swinging the ball from one side of his body to the other in one smooth, continuous sweeping movement. When that's completed he must face the goal in a good triple-threat stance.

The act of aggressively sweeping the ball, during which it will almost touch the court, forces the aggressive defender to anticipate the offensive player's dribble drive. In doing so the aggressive defender will take a step back in order to counter the sudden dribble-drive attack successfully.

Good Attacking Offensive Players Are Tight, Strong, and Low

A good attacking offensive player is always tight with the ball—which means keeping the ball in the shooting pocket or chinning it while it's in the player's possession. This habit makes it very difficult for the on-the-ball defender to strip the offensive player of the ball.

Good attacking offensive player must also be strong with the ball. He must hold the ball with hands on either side, increasing the firmness of his grip, again making it difficult for the on-the-ball defender to strip the ball from the offensive player.

A good attacking offensive player plays low. This refers to the stance he assumes. Offensive players who stand up straight when in possession of the ball have a more difficult time moving quickly and maintaining balance when pivoting or when under defensive pressure.

By staying low in a good offensive stance, the attacking player can pivot under pressure and maintain good balance and can quickly and suddenly attack the basket with a drive or explode upward for a jump shot. Playing low also allows the offensive player to absorb a foul and be able to finish a play, be it a shot or a pass.

The First Step Should Be Long, Low, and Straight

The first step of a dribble drive should be long, low, and straight. This principle helps the attacking offensive player maintain several other key offensive principles such as going somewhere with the dribble, driving to the goal from the three-point line in one dribble, and advancing the ball up the court in four dribbles.

If the attacking offensive player is being defended, the long, low first step helps him attack quickly. The long, low first step should reach at least as far as the foot of the defender being attacked, and it must be straight. This is in keeping with the principle of attacking in a straight line. If the first step is not straight, the attacking offensive player will move in a curve, allowing the defense an opportunity to recover.

If the first step is straight, the attacking offensive player should make some contact as he drives by the on-the-ball defender. Before an aggressive offensive player can attack, there must be bend in their knees to create the mechanical leverage necessary to explode on the driver. It simply is not possible to initiate an aggressive drive without the explosion created by this stance.

Players who establish the habit of aggressively facing up in triple threat also build the habit of being strong, tight, and low. These two habits ensure the attacking offensive player will have bend in his knees.

Move With a Purpose

Whether the offensive player has possession of the ball or not, he must move with a purpose in mind. This purpose must always be for the benefit of the team and its objectives as the team executes its strategy and tactics. Offensive movement without a purpose allows the defense not to defend the offensive player, giving the defense a numerical advantage over the offense.

Lower the Height of the Dribble As the Defensive Pressure Increases

The lower the ball is dribbled, the more control the ball handler will have, but he must advance slowly. The higher the

THE GAME OF BASKETBALL

ball is dribbled, the faster the ball handler can advance, but the less control of the ball he will have.

As the on-the-ball defensive pressure increases, the ball handler should dribble lower. This allows him to increase control of his dribble.

Pound the Ball When Dribbling

The ball handler only controls the ball when he is touching it. The harder the ball is dribbled, the sooner it will return to his hand. The less time in between moments of contact, the greater control of the ball the handler will have. Pounding the ball when dribbling ensures a rapid return of the ball to his hand.

Only Two Moves Are Needed: A Go-To Move and a Counter Move

The "less is more" concept certainly applies to basketball. An attacking offensive player needs two moves, no more. The first is a go-to move. This is the player's best offensive move and he must perfect it. The other move is the counter move to the go-to move. This allows the offensive player to attack the defense when the defense takes away the go-to move.

An example of this concept is the great dribble penetrator whose go-to move is the crossover dribble. When the on-the-ball defender successfully anticipates the crossover dribble move, the defender can suddenly change angle and take the crossover dribble away.

When this happens the dribble penetrator uses an in-out dribble move to attack. Instead of changing hands, as the dribble penetrator would on the crossover dribble, the dribble penetrator fakes the crossover move with the "in" dribble and then attacks without changing hands on the dribble move. The ball is moved in, giving the appearance of the first phase of the crossover, then out, allowing the dribble penetrator to keep the ball in the same hand after the defender has adjusted to take away the crossover dribble.

This concept applies to catch-and-shoot shooters and post players as well. The great catch-and-shoot three-point shooter's go-to move is to catch and shoot the three-point shot. The counter move is to shot fake and drive to the goal in one dribble. For the post player, the go-to move could be turn and shoot, and the counter move is the McHale move, also known as the *up and under*.

Use a Shot Fake to Take the Bend Out of the Defender's Knees

Just as the attacking offensive player must have bend in his knees in order to be explosive, on balance, and strong, so must the defender. The defensive player who stands up, taking the bend out of his knees, is at a big disadvantage when it's time to move quickly.

Every attacking offensive player has an objective of getting the on-the-ball defender to take the bend out of his knees, allowing the attacking offensive player to gain the advantage in explosiveness. The best way to do this is to use a simple, two-inch shot fake—as many as two or three if necessary. Aggressive defenders who lack discipline will often take the bend out of their knees on the first shot fake, thinking the offensive player is going to shoot. Even the disciplined on-the-ball defender will often succumb to a second or third shot fake; believing the offensive player is going to shoot on the third attempt, the defender will contest the shot.

Once the defender has taken the bend out of his knees, the attacking offensive player should execute a long, low, and straight first step, quickly and explosively driving past the defender.

Chapter Five

Playing the Post

Line of Deployment

Tex Winter, the master teacher of the triangle offense, teaches a concept called the *line of deployment*. An offensive post player must post up on the line of deployment in order to be both effective and open in an area where the post player can score. This imaginary line is between the rim and the ball, and the post player should straddle it, bisecting it at a ninety degree angle.

Post-Up Stance

The post-up stance is a variation of the basic athletic stance. The post player's legs must be slightly wider than hip width, with the knees bent at an angle between thirty and forty-five degrees, depending on the post player's build and size.

The back should be straight and strong, with the head centered between the knees and the chin level to the court. The elbows should be extensions of the shoulders, with the post player able to see the backs of the hands. The palms of the hands should be facing the ball, with the fingers pointed up and spread comfortably.

Arm and Leg Dominance

In order to be effective posting up or sealing, the offensive post player must establish both arm and leg dominance. This requires his leg to be physically over and on top of the post defender's leg. If the post defender attempts to defend on the post player's high side, his leg will be over the post player's high side leg. The offensive post player must move his high side leg over the post defender's leg, establishing leg dominance. This will allow the offensive post player to control the post defender's leg, thereby gaining a significant advantage in holding the desired post position.

Just as the post defender cannot be allowed to have leg dominance, the offensive post player cannot allow the post defender to have arm dominance. The offensive post player achieves arm dominance by obtaining the high position, meaning his arm is physically over the post defender's arm. The post defender must attempt to establish arm dominance in order to deflect any pass to the offensive post player. To prevent the post defender from gaining or regaining arm dominance, the offensive post player doesn't hold the post defender's arm but maintains a rigid position, not allowing the post defender to push, pull, or otherwise move the offensive post player's arm. This requires considerable strength in the upper back, shoulders, and arms on the part of the offensive post player.

Chin and Check Over the High Side Shoulder

Upon receiving the ball with both hands, the offensive post player chins the ball with both elbows pointing straight out as extensions of the shoulders, giving him great strength to maintain possession of the ball and prevent the costly mistake of lowering the ball to waist height, where it can be stripped.

After chinning the ball, the offensive post player must quickly look over his high side shoulder. This allows him to scan for all four offensive teammates and the five defenders. If he looks over the baseline shoulder, all he can see at best is the post defender, the baseline, and any player standing directly under the goal. A quick scan over the high shoulder provides the opportunity to see the greatest possible number of players and court area. If the offensive post player does not see the post defender, he can immediately make an offensive move to the middle of the lane.

It Must Take Two Defenders to Guard a Post

In order to contribute truly to the success of the team offense, an offensive low post player must be enough of a scoring threat to require two defenders. How the two defenders cover the offensive low post will vary, but generally there will be a post defender who has the primary responsibility of defending the offensive post player and an additional defender playing help defense in the lane behind the offensive post player.

By drawing two defensive players to the offensive post, the defense is at a numerical disadvantage somewhere on the court, usually on the help side perimeter. This allows the offensive team to place an excellent three-point shooter on the other side of the court, creating three-point shot opportunities.

Show Numbers

Post players must not only be on the line of deployment and generally in the post box or posting area; they must also show their numbers to the ball. Regardless of where the ball is on offense, the offensive post player on the ball side of the court must show his numbers to the ball. This allows the offensive player with the ball, usually on the perimeter, to best judge if the offensive post is open. If the numbers on the chest of the offensive post are clearly visible, the offensive player with the ball must pass it to him.

Go-To and Counter Move

Good post players who can score with great efficiency develop and perfect a go-to move, or a signature move. This is his favorite move, and he works hard to obtain the position that allows him to use the move as often as possible. Good post defenders work very hard to deny the offensive post player his desired post-up position and go-to move. When they are able to do this, the offensive post player must have a complimentary move. An example of a go-to post move is turning to the baseline and shooting, and the complimentary move is the McHale move to the middle of the lane.

Sprint the Floor

Post players can gain a significant advantage by sprinting the floor on each offensive possession. Having the discipline to carry out this simple concept on each offensive transition will result in two additional easy power post shoots. What player would not want to score four more easy points a game?

This tactic has the added benefit of producing considerable fatigue in the opposing post defender. Fatigued defenders commit more fouls, increasing the scoring opportunities for the post player. The opposing team suffers from the additional fouls added to the team foul totals.

Yet another added benefit of the post player sprinting the floor is the defense being forced to defend the rim and the area surrounding the goal. This allows teams with excellent three-point shooters to have opportunities in transition.

Need to Score

Post play is an intensely physical position. Teams must expend considerable energy on preventing offensive post players from obtaining excellent positions in areas on the court that result in high percentage shots. The limited available court space becomes congested with the number of bodies vying to occupy these positions, creating the inevitable physical contact and rough play that typifies post play.

Given the physical aspects of post play, both on offense and defense, and the importance of the offensive production that comes from the post, one of the most important traits a good offensive post player can have is an intense need to score. This provides the motivation the post player needs to sprint the floor on each possession, fight to post up, establish arm and leg dominance, hold a seal and maintain position, catch the ball in traffic, and, finally, score. The level of commitment required is high, and the physical exertion to play the post is considerable. Post players must have an intense need to score to make the commitment necessary and maintain it.

Pass Out and Reposition

Often, during the jostling that takes place in the post, the offensive post player loses the advantage of having the position to score after receiving the ball. This situation can easily be corrected by passing the ball back out to the perimeter quickly; as the defense relaxes while the ball is in flight to the perimeter player, the offensive post player regains the desired position and holds the seal. The second time the ball is entered into the offensive post, the defense usually is not able to gain the upper hand without fouling in the process.

Posting Area/Box

The posting area, sometimes referred to as a *posting box*, is the space on each side of the lane near the large square. Many post players make the mistake of posting up too low, or close to the baseline. When this happens, and they turn toward the baseline to shoot, there is very little room to use the backboard for a power shot inside. The posting area must be high enough up the lane so the offensive post player has adequate room to both maneuver and use the backboard effectively when executing post moves and power shots.

The most effective posting area is just below the first hash mark up, the lane line from the box on the lane. The offensive post player must establish his baseline foot here and be on the line of deployment. He must also show his numbers to the ball and establish and maintain arm and leg dominance.

Screen In Against the Zone

One of the most effective tactics an offensive post player can use against a zone is to take up position on the baseline behind the zone on the help side of the court. The offense can slide a three-point shooter down into the corner behind the post player. The offensive post player then sets a screen in against the last defender of the zone, usually in a defensive position in front of the rim.

The offense throws a skip pass across the zone defense, to the shooter in the corner behind the post player's screen. The last zone defender, regardless of the type of zone defense played, is responsible for covering the corner shooter. As the last defender fights over the post player's screen, the offensive post player aggressively moves to the next zone defender, executes a rear turn, and seals the next zone defender.

This tactic is excellent for obtaining three-point opportunities and creating an open passing lane into the offensive low post. The spacing obtained by the need to cover the three-point shooter and the offensive post player, sealing a post defender in what is usually the middle of the lane, creates an excellent post-entry passing opportunity.

High-Low Pass

The high-low pass, from the high post to the low post, is one of the most effective plays in basketball. This tactic can be made more effective if the pass from the high post player to the low post player is not made to the low post player but away from the defense. The pass should be flat, crisp, and just slightly above the reach of the low post offensive player when standing flat footed. The pass must be made in a line with the corner of the backboard.

By passing to this spot instead of directly to the low post offensive player, the low post defender and the help defender are taken out of the play, and the chances of the pass being deflected or intercepted are reduced. After receiving the pass, the low post offensive player, who had to jump to catch the pass, lands with feet pointing to the baseline and in position for a power shot.

Setting Up for a Lob

When the post defense plays the offensive post in such a way that a lob pass is available, the offensive post must turn his back to that of the post defender and, using his hips, seal the post defender out of the lane. The offensive post player must put both hands up, with elbows above eye level. This tactic prevents offensive fouls for pushing off when the lob pass is made.

This player must hold the position until the ball is directly over the offensive low post player's head, then he can release to receive the ball. The pass should be relatively flat and crisp, and above the reach of the post defender. The pass must be thrown to the corner of the backboard and not to the offensive post player. This prevents the defense from being able to position for drawing a charge off the unsuspecting offensive post player, who must focus on catching the ball and not on the help defense.

Chapter Six

For Coaches

TEAM Is the Most Important Thing

Mike Roller was the Lipscomb High School boys' varsity basketball coach when I first heard him give a lecture at a coaching clinic. His opening question had a profound impact on my coaching career.

Coach Roller asked what each coach present thought was the most important aspect of basketball. Answers ranged from fundamentals to defense. Coach Roller patiently listened to each coach and then informed everyone they were wrong.

"TEAM is the most important thing," he informed us. He was, and is, correct. Without a solid team concept and excellent interaction between everyone involved in the program, the group is doomed to be less successful, never to live up to its potential.

In addition the group will, in all likelihood, be full of strife and disagreements, and handicapped by its members' inability to deal positively with the adversity that comes to all groups during a season. Individual players will place their needs and desires before what is best for the team, ensuring the team will not succeed.

A losing season is not guaranteed if a group has a poor team attitude or team concept. But it will be a joyless season that lacks fun, excitement, and all the positives that make playing any team sport, basketball in particular, such a positive experience.

Even in a culture such as that of the United States, which places a heavy emphasis on individuality, players and coaches can be convinced that putting self aside for the benefit of the group is possible.

Working cooperatively in a group, by choice, for the benefit of all individuals involved is a critical component of success, particularly in the highly competitive US society. This might seem like a contradictory statement, but the individual who can set aside selfish or self-centered goals and ambitions, and utilize his skills for the benefit of the group, is almost always positively rewarded.

The concept of selfless thinking so the group can benefit is a key life skill that basketball can teach. It will serve players well later in life, when they become spouses, parents, business owners, or employees at large companies that utilize teams to complete projects.

The ultimate advantage of the team concept is that the players' skills are always greater when applied collectively, as a team, than when they attempt to apply their talents individually.

A simple illustration of this is to take a single twig and measure the effort required to break it. Take a dozen twigs of the same size and collect them into a bundle. Measure the effort required to break the bundle, if it is possible to do so. This is a simple but classic demonstration of why twelve players acting as a team are always better than twelve players acting as individuals.

Never Have an Easy Practice—Have a Short One

Basketball must be played with great intensity. The style or pace of play does not matter. Teams play like they practice. The logical extension of this concept is practice must be intense and demanding in order for teams to play with great effort and intensity during a game. Coaches will go to great lengths to create challenging practices.

However lurking in the shadows is a trap many coaches can fall into. Players only have so much gas in the tank. A season made up of long, relentlessly intense and demanding practices will result in a team that is spent mentally and physically at the most important point of the season: during league play and the state playoffs. Coaches who do not recognize this may make serious mistakes despite the best intentions.

In an effort to prevent burnout, some coaches make the mistake of having easy practices. This leads to poor game play. A team that has been conditioned to be intense and play hard will develop bad habits such as poor execution, decreased effort with the onset of fatigue, and making mistakes when confronted by an intense and aggressive opponent.

This all can be avoided by having shorter practices with the same level of intensity as early season practices. Players respond well to intense practices late in the season, particularly if they know in advance that if practice is intense and they execute well, they will be rewarded by having a short practice.

This approach is a win-win. By shortening practice, the risks of mental and physical burnout are lessened for the players and coaching staff. Continuing to have intense and physically demanding practices keeps the players sharp. Players generally prefer intense practices, especially when they feel like they have been rewarded for their intensity and effort.

A final benefit of this approach is that players will leave practice wishing they could have practiced a little bit longer. Mentally this helps them maintain their desire to succeed as the season winds down and draws to a close. This is particularly important for teams that are headed for the state playoffs, where intensity and passion make a huge difference in game outcomes.

A Day Off Can Be As Good As Having Practice

Coaches, by nature, are often workaholics. Players who love the game enjoy practicing, even practicing hard. But like a machine manufactured of the finest high-quality materials, there has to be time for scheduled maintenance or the machine will break down.

All too often coaches treat players as if they can run forever. However players, like machines, need scheduled maintenance. Unlike machines, oil and the replacement of key parts is not what players need.

Rest takes the place of maintenance for players. A break from the daily grind of practice is a positive in many ways. It allows the players downtime to do things they like but don't have time to do during the season.

A day off from practice can allow players to catch up or get ahead with schoolwork. Players with nagging injuries that won't go away can rest the body part or get extra treatment from the team trainer.

Doctor and orthodontist appointments for younger players who do not yet drive can be scheduled on days off. Knowing in advance when they'll have off allows parents to make such arrangements without causing the player to miss practice.

Best of all, from the player's perspective, a day off can provide a much-needed mental break from the stress of a long season and having to practice, prepare, and play at a high level each day.

Large companies long ago came to value the increase in productivity gained by having employees take regular vacations. Players, like employees, need regular breaks. Coaches can either include days off in the regular practice schedule or have surprise days off if the team needs a break from the routine. Experience will teach coaches when to provide the latter, particularly if practice has gotten stale.

If a day off cannot be provided, a good option is to have an intense practice that is very different from the normal routine. The dramatic change can be like a day off for players if the staleness and boredom are results of following the same routine too often.

Don't Give Orders That Can Be Understood; Give Orders That Cannot Be Misunderstood

This simple yet not easy quote is from American military leader Douglas MacArthur. It's a great lesson for any coach, and applies to any situation in which an individual is called upon to lead.

It's not enough to provide clear instructions to players in practice, team meetings, and games. The instructions must be of such a nature that players cannot misinterpret in any way what the coach requires of them.

Is there a more frustrating scenario than a player executing a play incorrectly at the end of a close game, particularly after a time-out where specific instructions were given, and as a result the game is lost? It's even more frustrating when the coach discovers the player did exactly what he thought was expected of him. The coach's instructions had two possible interpretations—the one the coach meant and what the player understood.

The player feels bad about the outcome of the game, and the coach is at risk of losing the respect of the other players, who might believe he did not know how to handle the situation.

To prevent such scenarios, coaches must learn how to give directions that cannot be misunderstood. This can be as simple as having players repeat the instructions he gives them or asking the players to explain what is intended by the instructions.

The coach can plan in advance for likely scenarios that can occur during a game. This approach allows for the preplanning of instructions, providing the coach time to evaluate the language he must use to ensure clarity and understanding on the part of the players.

You Don't Get Stronger by Picking Up Twigs, But You Can Break Your Back Picking Up Logs

The importance of scheduling properly is not taught in school. The right schedule can mean the difference between a successful, winning season and a demoralizing, losing season. Coaches often like to say they want to play as tough a schedule as possible before district play and then proceed to schedule their team into oblivion with overmatched opponents, one after another.

To be sure, some challenging games before the start of league play are essential. But a steady diet of games against teams that are significantly better will result in a spirit of defeatism and learned helplessness. Teams must have some success early in the season in order to believe in the system of offense and defense the coach is asking them to play, and to build confidence that they can win games.

Consider some easy opponents early in the season as twigs—your team won't get stronger picking up those wins. But your yard will certainly look much better in a short time as all of the twigs are cleaned up, leaving only the big limbs and a few logs to take care of. A team that is 8-2 going into a challenging tournament just before league play is more confident of success than a 3-7 team that has picked up the heavy branches and logs on the schedule.

Scheduling is a difficult area of coaching to master, and each coach must learn to get a feel for his own team's talent level and that of the available competition. Factors such as league play and rivalries must also be taken into consideration when scheduling.

Take the time and effort to craft an appropriate schedule for the coming season, balancing overmatched opponents with easy opponents. If you know you are going to lose, try to schedule the game for the opponent's gym, but be sure to balance that loss with a win on the road as well. Finally, make certain to schedule a reasonable number of games against opponents of similar strength and skill. Winning these games will build a winning team over the course of the season.

Fewer Rules Are Better—Be Flexible

The question each coach must answer concerning rules is simple: "Do I want to be a coach or a police officer?" It's important to realize that having a large number of rules will require considerable time and effort to police and enforce. A better approach is to have a limited number of broad rules that cover a wide range of situations a coach will face. For example "be on time" covers every possible situation involving a defined starting time.

State rules in a positive way when possible. Taking a positive stance when enforcing rules is more effective than taking a negative tone and will create better discipline. Wording rules in a positive tone helps to teach players what to do instead of focusing on what not to do. For example "be on time" is a positive way of communicating "do not be late."

The real objective is to begin each team function at the scheduled time. Focusing on being on time instead of not being late encourages proactive time management and helps players to arrive in a timely manner. An even better rule might be "be ten minutes early."

Have Your Captains Communicate Constantly With Officials

Officials are not inclined to talk to coaches during a game. In fact the rules state all communication must be through the team captain—understandable given the abuse most coaches direct at officials.

There are numerous positive reasons to have the captains communicate with the officials throughout the game. The first is simple: the rulebook states this is the proper method. Second it's a good learning experience for the captains. They need to learn to communicate effectively with adults in a wide range of situations. This is excellent practice!

Establishing positive communication via the captains throughout the entire game can be essential in the closing moments of a fiercely contested ball game. Officials are human and more likely to be communicative and responsive to the team that has communicated by the rules in a positive manner through the entire game. Never leave anything to chance.

The captains also act as a buffer for the coach during the emotional moments of a game. Establishing this method of communication forces the coach to temper his mood and ask questions or convey opinions in a tactful manner. This will carry over to the other members of the program.

Keep in mind that this is definitely a difficult area for nearly every coach in the profession, and it will take considerable work to adopt and perfect this approach.

Make the Off-Season Fun, But With a Purpose

The off-season is critical for the success of a basketball program. Yet for many players, off-season is something to be dreaded. To them, off-season work is sheer drudgery.

Some players are lazy, uncommitted, or so self-centered there is nothing a coach can do to change their views of off-season. These players can infect the rest of the team with their negative attitudes and do considerable harm to the program.

A proactive approach to off-season workouts can go a long way in preventing player dissatisfaction or complacency. Coaches forget all too soon what it was like to be a player. Players want to have fun with their sport. Making it into drudgery is a surefire way to kill player interest.

Organize a three-on-three league and let the players run and administer it. Make certain all workouts are tailored to the developmental needs of each individual player. This approach requires each player to be evaluated individually, and a workout specific to that player will be designed—a time-consuming process, but worth it.

Make certain everything done in the off-season relates directly to individual player and team goals and needs. Just as important is the need to educate each player and the entire group on the *why* behind everything and the benefit of each activity. Players are much more motivated when they understand the reasons for what is being asked of them. They need purpose to guide their efforts.

Every workout must be measurable, and players must be held accountable for keeping detailed, accurate records. Set short-term and long-term goals for the players and the team in regard to all off-season work.

Also keep your own records—the more detailed the better—of the team's and each player's progress. Post these records in public places, where the entire team and the general public can view their progress. This single act can do more than anything else to motivate a player or a team and to generate compliance with off-season expectations of the coaching staff.

Give awards for achievement in the off-season. The prizes can be determined by the players; they just need tangible rewards for the sacrifices and hard work they have invested in the off-season. Remember, a good number of players each year will not reap the rewards of their off-season work by increasing or receiving significant playing time. Rewards are especially important to these players.

Always find ways to make the off-season workouts fun, or at least bearable, for the players. Be creative, and ask for input from them; they often have the best ideas on how to make the off-season more fun. Always provide purpose to the workouts and communicate that purpose to the players.

Kill the Clock Simply by Running Your Regular Offense Without Shooting

Players have a great deal to keep track of. The less they have to think, and the more they are able to act correctly without thinking, the better. With this concept in mind, consider not having a delay game offense. This does not mean a team should go into a season without a method of running time off the clock. Instead spread the regular offense out a bit more and run it without taking any shot attempts.

In addition to reducing the amount the players have to remember, disguising a delay with this method can sometimes lull the opponent into not recognizing a delay offense is being run. Several minutes of game time can elapse before the opponent begins to implement a defensive strategy designed to counteract a delay offense. In a close game, losing several minutes when behind might be the difference in the outcome of the game. Disguising the delay offense might buy that needed time.

You Cannot Expect Your Players to Execute Something You Have Not Taught Them

Coaches have high expectations for their players in many different ways. It is both fair and just for coaches to demand that players meet or surpass those expectations. Failure to do so should have negative consequences for the players.

What is not fair is holding players accountable for something they did not know was expected of them or did not know how to carry out. Holding players accountable for these scenarios will serve only to discourage them and the team. With this in mind, coaches must hold themselves accountable for clearly and consistently communicating to their players and the team what is expected in every possible scenario and how to carry out the tasks to meet these expectations. When the coach has failed in this regard and a situation presents itself where the players are helpless due to a lack of foreknowledge, the coach must accept responsibility and let the players know they will not be held accountable.

Adherence to this principle goes a long way toward building trust and respect between players and the coach. Players are more accepting of high expectations when they know they will be held accountable in a just and fair manner and if they are clear on what is expected.

When Throwing a Length-of-the-Court Pass

Games have been lost due to the clock running off one or two precious seconds at the end. Rather than wasting those precious seconds due to a mistake either deliberate of accidental, control the situation by communicating a polite and brief reminder to the officials about the rules regarding clock management. It is then their responsibility monitor the clock operator in these important final seconds of the game.

Less Is More—When You Add Something, You Must Take Something Away

Players can only retain so much information. The more a player has to recall before being able to act during a game, the more time it will take him to act. The split second lost on extra processing might be the difference between drawing a charge and committing a blocking foul, passing for a layup or committing a turnover.

Teams and players reach a saturation point during a season. Anything added to the required set of facts and rules will slow the player and the team down. When it is necessary to add a new play or wrinkle to the defensive scheme, it is necessary to take something away from the total body of knowledge the player is required to master.

By subtracting one item from the system, another item can be added. Think of a suitcase that has been packed to capacity. Adding one more item will cause it to burst. In order to add the additional item, one item of similar size must first be removed.

When Selecting Your Team, Keep Two Character Players on the Roster—Cut All of the Problem Attitudes

It's better to have fifteen minutes of agony and not suffer a season of pain. Always cut players with bad attitudes. No player, no matter how talented, is bigger than the team or the program. Keeping those with bad attitudes on the team roster will create discipline problems that will create a negative atmosphere for the entire team.

John Wooden believed it was not possible to have an entire roster of talented players who were capable of starting *and* have a positive team environment. There had to be players who understood their roles as practice players. Wooden believed these character players are just as important as the star players because they make it possible to have a well-balanced team that's able to practice and work well together for the duration of the season.

The More Talented Your Players Are, the More Restrictions You Will Need on Offense

Dean Smith of the University of North Carolina was one of the greatest recruiters in the history of college basketball. The Tar Heels routinely had a roster full of high school All-Americans and future NBA All-Stars.

These players were so gifted and athletic, it was possible for any of them, at any given time, simply to step outside the team concept and play one on one and have success.

This individual approach might result in impressive stats for a particular player, but ultimately it will lead to failure for the team. To Coach Smith the most important thing, which would lead to success for the team *and* the individual players, is putting the team first.

In order to ensure these players stayed within the team framework and used their impressive individual talents only for the benefit of the team, Coach Smith built restrictions into the offense. They limited the players just enough to force them to subjugate their skills to the offensive framework, yet in such a way the players retained their individual initiative and confidence in their abilities.

An example of Coach Smith's restrictions was the requirement that before any UNC player shot or dribbled the ball, he first had to hold it over his head while facing the goal. This simple habit prevented players from consistently shooting or driving as soon as they caught the basketball.

The Less Talented Your Players Are, the More Freedom They Will Need on Offense

Just as more-talented players need restrictions to limit them to the team concept, less-talented players will need more freedom in order to have success. When facing an athletic opponent, less-talented teams can often be prevented from running their offensive sets by the opponent's aggressive denial or trapping defense.

Players with less talent must be allowed more freedom in these situations in order to escape the pressure and have a chance of success. Forcing less-talented players into a restrictive pattern of play allows the more-athletic team to dictate exactly how the game will be played. The less-talented player will not be able to overcome the athleticism of the other team or player, and forcing him to run a restricted system of play will inevitably lead to mistakes.

Only Give Players One Concept to Focus on During a Time-Out, and Make It the Last Thing They Hear

Players view time-outs as periods to rest, catch their breath, and drink some fluids. Coaches view time-outs as a means to change momentum in the game and convey important information to the players.

Both groups are correct. With this in mind, coaches must limit the information they communicate to one item. Players can only take in a limited amount while they are trying to rest, rehydrate, and regain their composure.

Players will remember the last piece of information the coach gives them during the time-out, so the coach must make certain to communicate what's most important as the time-out ends.

Respect the Practice Schedule and Calendar—Players Have Lives Outside the Game

Coaching is not a profession for clock watchers. Individuals who are not willing to work long, hard hours should not enter the coaching profession.

While this may be true for coaches, it is not true for players. Coaches need to remember players are kids and have lives outside of the game. They play for fun and to belong to a group.

Unless they are one of the very few who go on to play their sport for money, it is not their job.

Coaches need to honor the practice and game schedule. When it is the scheduled time to end practice, the players need to be released. Practices should not be added to the schedule. It is better to schedule every possible practice that could be needed and then cancel some than to try to add practices.

When the coach honors the schedule's time commitments, players and their families are able to plan their other activities. In turn this allows the coach to expect players and families to honor the team's schedule.

Players' Appearances Must Be Uniform for Games—If They Don't Look Like a Team They Won't Play Like a Team

The most important concept in this sport is being a team. Nothing shouts "I am an individual" more than one player refusing to conform to the team image in terms of dress.

Players must be uniform in their appearance for games. The power of this visual image goes a long way toward imposing the team concept on what would otherwise be a collection of individuals. This approach tells each player that he belongs to the team. The unified visual image conveys single-mindedness of purpose to the opponent.

Insist Players Use the Glass on Layups

Free throws and layups are how teams win games. This includes teams that rely heavily on the three-point shot.

Since layups are such an important factor in determining the outcome of a game, the coach must insist his players use the most effective method of shooting them, thereby increasing the chances of success for both the individual and the team.

The most effective method is to kiss the ball high and soft off the glass, using the square painted on the backboard as a guide. Any player who refuses to follow this mandate should simply have a seat for the duration of the game.

Practice One Special Situation Each Day in Practice

The majority of games are decided by just a few points. For many teams the successful execution of so-called special situations at the conclusions of games lead to victory.

While both teams will play the bulk of the game will be with the normal offense and defense, the execution of the special situation concepts can be the deciding factor. There are simply too many possible variables to have a preplanned offense or defense for each of the possible special situations. With this in mind, well-prepared coaches take the time to plan a general approach for as many special situations as possible.

A few minutes of every practice should be allotted to work on a special situation. By taking the general, well-planned framework and adapting it to the situation of the day, coaches can prepare their teams to handle nearly any situation that might arise during a game.

The daily practice of something unusual, requiring adaption on the spot in order to achieve success, teaches players how to do just that during the final moments of a game.

The Only Way to Get Better Is to Work at It

Coaches often make the mistake of thinking they have learned all they need to know about their profession and their sport. However coaches, like players, must improve. The only way a coach can improve is to work at it, just like players do.

Mentally Tough Coaches Coach Through Poor Officiating

The quality of officiating can have an impact on coaches just as it does on players. A tough coach is able to maintain mental and emotional control when the officiating is less than perfect or when a critical juncture of the game goes against the coach's team.

Once an official has made a call, nearly ninety-nine percent of the time it will not be reversed. The coach must be aware of what is a correctable error and accept that the rest of the time the mistake or poor call will stand. A coach must also be aware that many times the official is correct, and the player was guilty of the infraction as called.

Mental toughness during this type of adverse situation has many positive consequences. The coach will be better able to make a proactive, positive, and correct decision for his team. His attitude will be reflected by the team and possibly even the fans.

A coach does not have control over the actions of officials and thus should not be concerned with them. It is far more productive for the coach to focus on what he can control. It requires mental toughness to adopt this approach, but the benefits of controlling what can be controlled and ignoring the rest are considerable.

It Is Better for Players to Be Slightly Under-conditioned but Mentally Fresh Late in the Season

Weapon makers learned long ago that if too fine a point is honed on the edge of a sword, the metal could break when it comes into contact with another hard object. The sword blade has to contain both hard and soft steel in order to be functional—the hard to hold the edge of the weapon and the soft to allow the blade to absorb the energy from the impact of another weapon, so the blade doesn't shatter.

The same is true of athletes in a physically demanding sport, such as basketball, that has a long season. Basketball players must be well conditioned in order to compete at a high level and be able to avoid injury. Yet if athletes are over-conditioned, they become susceptible to injury and mental burnout.

None other than the great John Wooden himself believed it was better to slightly under-condition players. Over the course of the season this would allow them to remain fresh, preventing mental staleness, cumulative physical fatigue, and injury.

If Your Gym Has Only One Scoreboard, Position Your Bench to Face It in the Second Half

Many gyms, for a variety of reasons, have only one scoreboard. If this is true of your facility, or if you are playing in such a facility in a tournament, be certain to occupy the bench that is opposite the scoreboard.

This practice will allow the point guard to see the scoreboard and thus be aware of the time and score without having to turn his head to do so. In a close game, one turnover resulting from such a head turn could be the difference between victory and defeat.

A Team Takes on the Personality of Its Coach—Be Calm and Confident Under Pressure

Teams tend to take on the personalities of their coaches to some degree or another. For this reason it is important always to remain calm and composed during a game. Coaching with intensity is fine—in fact desirable—so long as it is controlled.

When the inevitable adversity comes during the game, players look to their coach to measure the situation they are facing. A calm, controlled presence on the sideline will extend to the players, helping them deal with the situation.

The same is true when the team is facing an ongoing crisis that extends for several days or weeks. If the head coach is able to deal with the challenging situation in a controlled and positive manner, it will help the players react the same way.

Free Throws and Layups Win Games

As coaches we all have egos, and some are larger than others. We like to think our special offense or defense wins games—or, better yet, the last-minute adjustment we make during a timeout.

The truth is our players' abilities to make free throws and layups during games decide the outcome of fiercely contested, close ball games. Dunks and three-point shots are certainly crowd pleasers, and the three-point shot has revolutionized the game today. But the lowly free throw and layup decide the outcomes.

If you disagree with this statement, take your scorebooks from past seasons and check the stats for the games your team lost by five points or fewer. The first stat you should check is how many free throws your team missed. The second is how many of those free throws were the first of a one-and-one opportunity.

Next check your shot chart for the game. How many layups were missed? In a five-point loss, one layup and three free throws are the difference between overtime and a possible win, and the loss your team suffered.

If you still aren't convinced, consider this scenario: Your team made the layup and one of the free throws. If you are able to take the last shot of the game instead of trailing by five points with no hope to win, a three-point shot or play will do it, and a two-point shot can send the game into overtime. Nothing has changed other than your players making one more free throw and one more layup. Your team did not force an additional turnover or turn the ball over one less time. You did not get a single additional shot attempt of any kind. You simply made a layup and one additional free throw.

You must create a culture within the team that places a heavy premium on making every layup attempted and encourages the team to have an average shooting percentage of seventy percent or better from the foul line. It is not enough just to tell the players about the importance of making their free throws and layups. They must practice them in game-like conditions. Players will do and value what their coach emphasizes, not what their coach talks about.

Be sure to practice free throws with fresh legs and an emphasis on technique. Practicing when the players are tired makes them more likely to make mistakes in execution.

Have your players practice layups from every conceivable angle of approach that can take place during a game. The worst possible drill for practicing layups is one nearly every coach uses: two line layups. How often do players shoot layups from those exact angles in a game?

Chapter Seven
Fouls and Such

Drawing the Charge

The single best play in the game of basketball is to draw the charge. This is a concept that bears repeating many times. The simple act of drawing a charge adds one foul to the total of the individual who committed the charge; it adds one foul to the opponent's team foul total; it can negate a basket; and the team that took the charge is rewarded possession of the ball.

Play Until the Whistle Blows

The referee's whistle, and nothing else, controls when play stops. The horn sounding does not stop play. A player traveling does not stop play. The ball going out of bounds does not stop play. Only the sound of the official's whistle can stop play.

With this concept in mind, players should be conditioned mentally to play until they hear the whistle. Unless the official blows the whistle to indicate the ball has gone out of bounds, a traveling violation has occurred, or a foul has been committed, play should continue. Teams that are conditioned to follow this concept will take advantage of those odd situations in which the official misses an obvious call and the other team stops, thinking play will be stopped. Take advantage of this rule by conditioning your players not to stop until the whistle blows, particularly when a foul has been committed.

Get to the Foul Line

One of the most important things for a team to do is get to the foul line to shoot free throws. This allows them to score with the clock stopped, substitute after a made free throw, and set up a pressing defense if so desired. It also means yet another foul has been added to the individual total of one of the opponent's players as well as the opponent team's total. The more fouls the opponent commits, the more its options are limited as the game progresses.

Ability to Draw a Foul

The ability to draw a foul is essential for a player and a team to develop. The player who can draw fouls successfully will create easy scoring opportunities as the game progresses. The opponent either will grow weary of fouling or will not be able to foul due to foul totals, allowing the individual player to drive to the goal for easy shots or to shoot open uncontested shots.

The ability to draw a foul is also a critical component of the strategy of getting to the foul line as a team. The two easiest techniques to draw a foul are the shot fake and penetration to the goal either by the dribble or with a pass to a player in the post area.

Help the Player You Have Just Fouled Stand Up

There are lots of reasons to follow this simple rule. First it's the right thing to do. Second it prevents a lot of unnecessary anger and hostility from building up between two players and their teams. Nothing can diffuse a potentially explosive situation like a good display of sportsmanship. The third reason is to never give the opponent a reason to play with more intensity and passion. Again, good sportsmanship can diffuse many tense situations.

Foul Only for Profit

Most coaches don't give a lot of thought to fouling, other than they don't want their players to do it or when to foul if they're behind late in a game. This is a dangerous mistake. Coaches should give considerable thought to the entire concept of fouling.

The wisest course of action involves a view of fouling that is incorporated into the team's philosophy, particularly in the areas of defense, rebounding, and offensive charging. Simply stated, this concept is to *foul only for profit*. The lone exception to this is smart hustle fouls, which can be defined as diving for a loose ball, fighting for a rebound when neither rebounder has a clear positional advantage, attempting to draw a charge, and only drawing these fouls when it does not place the player's team in a negative situation, the bonus, or the double bonus free throw shooting situation.

Never Allow the Opponent to Shoot a One-and-One Unless You Want Him To

This concept is more clearly defined by saying the opponent should never shoot a bonus free throw, a one-and-one, or double bonus unless deliberately forced to do so. Fouling should always be viewed as a mistake and treated accordingly unless it is a smart hustle foul.

Avoid Fouling by Focusing on Technique and Position

Teams that play aggressive man-to-man or an aggressive trapping defense often commit a large number of fouls, sometimes to the detriment of their style of play. This could be avoided by placing a heavy teaching emphasis on footwork, positioning, angles, and hand discipline. Teams that are in position defensively, take the correct angles, use the correct defensive technique and footwork, and do not reach will commit a low number of fouls.

An examination of most defensive fouls will show most are committed due to lack of discipline, lack of hustle covered up with a reach, simply reaching, attempting to block a shot, being out of position, etc. In other words most defensive fouls are preventable! The same is true for rebounding fouls, offensive charging fouls, and fouls in general.

It is worth the effort to teach players that fouling is one of the most heinous things they can do during a game. This does not mean they must be passive; it simply means they must hustle more, be disciplined, learn technique, and actually play defense and rebound like they should! This requires a great deal of effort on the coaching staff's part, but it is worth it.

Think of the advantage of the opponent never going to the foul line for a one-and-one. How many points does this take from them? For some teams it could be as much as one third of average offensive production. Think of the frustration this can cause and the negative impact on the opposing coach's relationship with the officials. It could create a crybaby atmosphere, and the opponents may shift their focus to the officials instead of executing their game plan.

Foul to Win

Having talked about the importance of not fouling, now we can look at the times when it's appropriate to foul. Many such instances require that the opponent *not* be in the bonus situation! How many games have been lost in the final seconds because the defensive team did not foul the offensive team before the ball could be advanced across half-court, or entered into an offensive set or a special play run? A foul in that situation would have put the offensive team on the foul line, and this is to be avoided. The disciplined defensive team that does not foul may have several fouls to give in this situation before the limit is reached and the bonus free throws are awarded. With two or three fouls to give, as much as ten seconds can be run off the clock, drastically limiting the opponent's opportunity to obtain a quality shot.

Foul Early

Another situation to foul for profit is one coaches seldom think about. When trailing late in the third quarter, if a team has committed few or no fouls, it might be wise to commit several fouls intentionally to raise the total number of team fouls to five. This leaves a little margin for error, and if it is necessary to foul and force the opponent to the foul line to obtain possession of the ball, time will not be wasted committing fouls to reach the bonus.

In addition to saving valuable time late in the game, there is a psychological advantage to this approach. It clearly sends a signal early in the second half that while the team committing the fouls may be trailing, they are going to make an aggressive run, and this may cause the team being fouled to lose some confidence.

Teach Players to Steal

Players must be trained how to foul so intentional fouls can be avoided. It's a wise idea to spend one minute each practice working on fouling for profit, or deliberately fouling. This allows a team to become efficient in this skill, which saves valuable game time and prevents unnecessary intentional fouls from being called. It also allows the offensive unit to work on handling the situation, making them more confident when finishing out a close game.

It's important to emphasize two concepts when fouling. The first is to always play the ball. This is the key factor in preventing the intentional foul call, and often the ball will pop loose as a result, no foul will be called, and the defense can go over to the offensive for a potential fast-break scoring opportunity. The second concept is to always play until the whistle blows. Just because the team is fouling for profit does not mean a ball may pop loose as a result of contact and an official might not call the foul. All too often this happens and an opportunity to score is lost.

It Takes a Thief

A sound concept to practice is the use of a designated fouler. The ideal player for this spot would be in the rotation and solid on both defense and offense, but not contributing much to the team's scoring total. This type of designated fouler has the advantage of being more confident due to regular playing time and is less likely to make a costly error on offense or defense. If all of the players in the rotation are needed, it is wise to have a designated fouler who understands exactly what is expected when he's called upon to fulfill this role.

By designating particular players as foulers, the role of who is to carry out this task is well defined, which will go a long way toward preventing key offensive or defensive players from picking up fouls that could prove costly in the late stages of the contest. It is also a good way to rest key offensive or defensive players. The designated fouler enters the game so the key player can both rest and not pick up fouls.

Scouting and Planning in Advance to Foul

Who to foul is a difficult question best answered by what is going on at the moment in the game—whether the fouling team is ahead or behind, and who is playing for the opponent.

If the fouling team is ahead by a slim margin, the game is in its concluding moment, and the trailing team is *not* in the bonus, it is a good idea to foul the trailing team's playmaker as soon as he obtains possession of the ball.

This accomplishes several positive things at once. It forces the opponent to take the ball out of bounds, allowing the fouling team to set its defense and force the opponent to struggle once again just to get the ball in bounds, creating more mental pressure. It takes the ball out of the hands of the playmaker at least for the time being, and hopefully places it into the hands of a less skilled and less confident player who may turn it over. The act of being fouled, especially if the fouling team has several fouls to give, may unnerve the playmaker, who knows he is likely to receive repeated fouls. Lastly if the ball is being inbounded in the backcourt, it allows the fouling team to turn up the pressure defensively.

Deliberately fouling a great shooter, even if the opponent is in the bonus, is an option that should be considered. If the game is in its final seconds, under ten, and the opponent is down by three or more points, it is worth considering fouling the opponent's best three-point shooter the instant he catches the ball. This eliminates the possibility of a successful three-point field goal attempt and means the fouling team will gain possession of the ball and the lead.

The drawback to this approach is if the shooter gets the field goal attempt off before the foul can be committed while still on the floor. Three free throws will be awarded, which could tie the contest, or worse still the attempt could go in and a free throw could be awarded, which could result in the opponent taking the lead. The opponent could make the first free throw, miss the second, and obtain the offensive rebound and score either a two or three-point goal.

This also might not be a wise strategy if the opponent has come from behind by pressing and has had success forcing turnovers on inbounds passes late in the game. Even if the shooter makes both of the two free throws, the fouling team must now inbounds the ball successfully in a situation in which it has recently experienced failure.

If a detailed scouting report is available, or the opponent is well known, it might be wise to foul at a key juncture in a set play that often results in an easy basket for the opponent. This prevents the opponent from scoring and forces them to inbounds the ball, using up more valuable clock, and it may even cause the opponent to change the play.

When fouling while behind in an effort to force the opponent to shoot free throws to relinquish possession of the ball, it is key that the recipients of the foul are not the strongest free-throw shooters. Most well-coached teams will take their weakest foul shooters out of the game to prevent this from happening, so it's important to have a well-defined idea of who to foul, and this information must be communicated to the players.

The best time to foul for profit when behind is in a deadball situation. This creates a free-throw opportunity without any time elapsing. The ball does not need to be inbounded. The foul could be committed on a screen, or by stepping into the path of a cutter. In fact this is the ideal time to be able to control *who* is fouled because ball is not in play.

Chapter Eight

Time-Outs

Using Time-Outs

There is nothing magical about time-outs. They are valuable if used properly, but they are not the sole means of controlling a game, resting players, or communicating with players. Always keep in mind that proper before-hand preparation is the real key to handling close situations in a tight game, not last-minute instructions in a time-out.

Having said that, there are some valuable uses for time-outs, and they are worth using wisely. In order for a time-out to be effective, a coach must keep several things in mind. The first is that only the players will retain only a limited amount of information from the time-out. The second is that the attitude the coach projects during the time-out, particularly in the final stages of a close game, is important to how the players come out of a time-out and play. Time-outs can be used to rest players, break an opponent's momentum, calm down a shaken team, convey communication, attempt to rattle an opponent, make substitutions, review how situations should be handled, and, if necessary, prepare for a final possession of a game.

Have a Routine to Maximize Each Time-Out

Having and following a routine for each time-out is important. Some teams like to take their time-outs away from the bench. There are good reasons to do this. The first is to reduce the noise level so the players can hear in a loud gym. The second reason is eliminate human distractions. Sad to say, but parents, friends, fans, and others can prevent a player from focusing on the time-out.

For a thirty-second time-out, it is advisable to stand. A full time-out might allow enough time to bring out chairs for the players to sit down. Only bring chairs onto the playing court if no substitutions are going to be made and the players need to be rested.

In order to maximize the time-out, the players on the court need to be trained to hustle over to the bench. The players not currently in the ballgame need to form a circular wall around the five players who will be playing, both to eliminate distractions and to hear clearly, like the five who will enter the game.

In the first ten to fifteen seconds of the time-out, regardless of the time-out's total length, the coaching staff should allow the players to catch their breath, calm down, drink water, wipe themselves off, and clear their minds so they can focus on what the staff will tell them. The coaches should use those seconds to decide what information to focus the players' attention on. Once it's time to communicate to the players, only the head coach should speak, making it possible for the players to focus their attention on one source of information. The players should then break and hustle out on the court.

Communication and the Time-Out

In the case of a thirty-second time-out, the coaching staff should attempt to communicate only one major concept. Usually that is all the players will retain, and this way all the players will be focused on the same single concept.

In a full time-out, the coaches can communicate more information. A suggested format is to take the first ten to fifteen seconds to let the players relax while the coaches meet. Then the assistant coaches or student assistant coaches can relay vital information to individual players, such as a foul total or individual instruction. This should take no more than ten seconds. Then the focus should be on the head coach, who will communicate the concluding information of the time-out. In a full time-out, it's possible to review several pieces of information, but always remember that the last concept presented will be the one the players are most likely to remember.

If time permits it's also a good idea to let the players ask questions or make suggestions. This does not mean the time-out is a town meeting complete with votes, but it is always wise to listen to players—especially those who are experienced—during a game.

A well-prepared team that is victorious in a close game that goes down to the final seconds walks off the court with several time-outs remaining. This indicates that the team was prepared for all the situations it faced and dealt with them successfully.

Conserve Time-Outs and Use Them Wisely

Even the most well prepared team may need all of its time-outs in a closely contested game to achieve victory. The legendary University of North Carolina head coach Dean Smith was noted by his desire to hoard time-outs in the event that they would be needed at the end of the game. Given the number of times that Coach Smith successfully utilized these hoarded time-outs to guide his team to victory, it is a good indication that a similar practice would be wise for other coaches.

Planning in Advance and Preparation in Practice Is Better

If it is a given that time-outs should be used wisely, when and who should call them? As a general rule, only the head coach should ever call a time-out, although there are several situations in which the players should be given the freedom to call time-outs on their own, without input from the head coach.

Teach Players the Good Reasons to Call Time-Outs and When to Do So

Just when should a player have the discretion to call a time-out? The answer often depends on time and score, the stage of the game, and the number of time-outs remaining for the team. A very silly use is when players attempt to save a ball from going out of bounds by calling a time-out, to prevent a violation from being called. Unless it is in the final minutes of a close game, this is one of the worst possible uses of a time-out.

The only time a player should use a time-out for this is if the game is at the stage where every single possession of the ball is of paramount importance. For example the player who calls the time-out in this situation has made a good play if his team is down by two points with eighteen seconds remaining. The upcoming single possession may allow his team to score a goal that will either tie the game or put his team up by a single point. To make this situation clear for players, it is wise to institute a rule that calling a time-out is permissible in this scenario only if there are less than two minutes and only two time-outs remaining in the game. If it there is less than one minute remaining, it is acceptable to call a time-out. Otherwise, calling a time-out to prevent an out-of-bounds violation is a serious mistake.

The same serious mistake can be made when a player calls a time-out to prevent a jump ball from being called. Again there is a scenario when this is acceptable. If the opponent has the arrow in the alternating possession, and there is less than a minute remaining (each coach can determine how much time on the clock is acceptable for the player to call time-out), it is a good use of a time-out as it will allow continued possession of the ball. If the arrow is in the direction of the team that calls the time-out, it's a mistake to do so as possession of the ball will be retained anyhow.

To Let Players Call Time-Outs or Not—That Is the Question

While it's a good general rule not to give players the freedom to call time-outs at their discretion, there are times when this form of player autonomy is essential. First the coach must spend time instructing the player on the time, score, and situation in which this power is theirs. Failure to do so is setting the player up to fail.

Only two players should be given the autonomy to call time-outs: the designated inbounder and the point guard. In the case of the designated inbounder, the responsibility to make this decision comes late in the game, when facing a pressure defense that is preventing the ball from being inbounded. In this instance the inbounder must have the freedom to realize that the ball cannot be successfully inbounded, and, if the time-outs remaining allow it, call one. It is wise to train the inbounder to inform the official prior to receiving the ball on a dead ball that if the count reaches four, the inbounder intends to call a time-out. It is also essential for the team captain or the inbounder, when the opportunity presents itself late in the game, to inform both officials that if the opponent scores and applies a pressure defense full court, if the inbounder cannot inbounds the ball by the four count, he will call a time-out. This simple act of communication ensures nothing unfortunate will happen in terms of a violation being called.

A point guard might call a time-out late in the game if he does not recognize a defense the team must attack, particularly if protecting a slim lead. Calling a time-out to prevent a turnover by a weak player, a double team of a weak player or of any player in a unfavorable location on the court, or to prevent a weak free throw shooter from being fouled is also acceptable.

For this type of autonomy to be effective, these players must be well schooled in time and score situations and have made these decisions in practice sessions prior to a game. They must also be aware of how many time-outs are remaining, and if that number allows them to call another. It is the responsibility of either the coaching staff or the student assistants to communicate this information constantly to these two key positional players during the course of a game.

Have a Strategy or Plan for Using Time-Outs

When should the coach call a time-out? Many will do so to break the opponent's momentum, and this is certainly an appropriate use. Substitutions are another way to accomplish the same goal. By substituting one or two players every dead ball for a minute, it might be possible to save the time-out for later and, by disrupting the flow of the contest, break the opponent's momentum at that time.

As a general rule, a coach should instruct his team in the strategies or tactics they must be able to execute in order to successfully attack anything the opponent throws at them. Sometimes, despite excellent scouting, planning, and practice preparation, the opponent successfully catches a team unprepared and is able to temporarily overwhelm them. In this instance there is no choice except to call a time-out, calm the players, and provide instruction—though remember players will remember only one or two things at best, so provide only key information.

There are some games, though, when the floodgates just open. Even though it is a general rule to attempt to conserve time-outs for the end of a game, if the opponent is so far ahead that a comeback is not possible, the time-outs will serve no constructive purpose, so a coach should go ahead and use as many as it takes to stop the flood waters.

It does bear mentioning that in certain situations it is fairly obvious a coach should call a time-out—for example to ice the opponent who is about to shoot a critical free throw, or after a final made free throw in order to set up a press.

When Not to Call a Time-Out

Not many coaches stop and think about the situations in which it would be better not to call a time-out—such as when doing so allows the opposing coach to organize how he wants to deal with the situation and remind his players of different bits of information, tactics, or strategies. Why allow the opponent this luxury?

There are certain situations that are key and can be rehearsed over and over well in advance so that when one takes place in a game, the players know exactly what to do and do not need a time-out.

One example of when not to call a time-out is when the opponent scores with ten seconds or less and the score is tied or the opponent is ahead by one or two points. If four or fewer seconds remain on the clock, it is necessary to call a time-out and run a special full-court play in this scenario. However most teams, particularly at the high school and junior high levels, are so happy to have a scored that the players simply get back and hope the opponent does not score.

In this scenario instruct your designated inbounder to inbounds the ball as quickly as possible to the point guard, who will drive straight to the goal. The best shooters should take positions on both wings and the low post player should run to the low post opposite the point guard. Many teams will simply let the point guard score, or foul him in the act of driving or shooting. Well-coached teams may collapse and force a pass, which is fine as the play has been rehearsed and the shooters have run to positions where they are capable of scoring. If a time-out is *not* called, chaos may prevail, resulting in an easy score.

Should the opponent be up by a three-point goal, it might be wise to inbounds the ball and have the point guard drive it hard to the bench area, and call a time-out to set up a side-out-of-bounds play designed to obtain a three-point shot.

When the Other Coach Calls a Time-Out

A major area that many coaches overlook is what to consider when the opposing coach calls a time-out. The "one or two trips only" strategy is excellent: if a 1-2-1-1 zone press has been effective, consider coming out of the time-out and employing a full-court pressure, man-to-man defense for one or two defensive possessions only. The idea behind this is that whatever instructions the opposing coach gave will be ineffective against the changed defense, in this case from a zone press to a man-to-man press, and after one or two trips the original defensive strategy or tactic can once again be utilized effectively, as the opposing players will have forgotten the instructions their coach gave them.

In addition when the opposing coach calls a time-out, or during any time-out for that matter, a coach can make a substitution to confuse matchups or create a possible mismatch.

The final suggestion concerning time-outs is yet another that many coaches do not consider: sometimes it is fine simply to call a time-out and review things, talk things over, and give the players a chance to catch their breath. This is particularly useful with about four minutes left in a game that gives every indication it will be close, or not decided until the final possession. Often the opposing coach will not think that far ahead, and it is wise to rest key players and review with them what to expect as they close the game out.

Chapter Nine

Some Game Tactics

Use a Designated Inbounder

Experience has taught that designating players as inbounders is essential. This is true in all three of the situations wherein a team must inbounds a basketball: after a made basket or free throw, in a baseline out-of-bounds situation, or in a sideline out-of-bounds situation.

Designated inbounders must be able to:

- make mental decisions with quarterback speed.
- handle the ball at least three dribbles without turning it over, whether under defensive pressure or not.
- read defenses.
- pass the ball accurately and away from the defense.
- pass the ball the length of the court with reasonable accuracy.
- handle mental pressure as well as, if not better than, the point guard.
- While not required, it really helps if the designated inbounder:
    - is a post player.
    - can shoot and make the three-point shot from the top of the key area.
    - is a pitcher on a baseball team.

A designated inbounder can take advantage of many easy scoring opportunities. Two designated players can be coached to look for a wide range of opportunities; it would be hard to instill this ability in all the players. Using a designated inbounder not only allows a team to take advantage of opportunities when they present themselves but reduces turnovers as a result of utilizing random inbound passers.

The designated inbounder must learn to treat a made basket like a rebound following a made basket, taking the ball out six inches below the net. He must tuck the ball into the throwing pocket over his shoulder, by his face. When taking the ball out of the net, the inbounder must stand on his right foot. When reading the pass, he must take three steps out of bounds to the right side of the backboard, to avoid hitting it when throwing a long pass.

Going Long Following a Made Basket or Against a Pressing Defense

While this twist can be used regardless of offensive approach, it is most effective when used by a team that fast breaks on every change of possession. A numbered break that assigns players to lanes is the easiest system for players to learn.

Many teams will celebrate after scoring, particularly late in a game after a difficult possession, often resulting in a slower than normal defensive transition. By sprinting two players up the sidelines, it is possible to throw the long pass for an easy score while the defense celebrates. The easy score in this situation is devastating for the opponent.

A long pass is a good way to beat man-to-man presses that play tough denial defense. Simply throw the long pass down court over both the offensive and defensive players' heads, targeted to bounce on the corner of the foul line on the side of the receiver's inside shoulder. The defender's position is made worse if the cutter breaks toward the inbounder, then goes deep. The inbounder must read to make certain there is no centerfield defender, or the deep offensive player must cut to the inbounder to clear the defense. One or two quick home run passes in succession can get a team out of its press in a hurry.

If a team does not press and does a decent job of getting back defensively by running numbered breaks on made baskets, it is possible to create other quick scoring opportunities. Throwing the pass to a sideline cutter who pulls up outside the three-point line will quickly pull defenders out to the ball, creating an opportunity for penetration with the dribble or to feed the post player who has sprinted to the rim. Either of these opportunities is highly likely to result in an old fashioned three-point play due to the defense fouling as a result of poor positioning and surprise.

Developing a reputation for throwing long balls in games can have a positive impact on how the opponent plays your team. Going long can get pressing teams not to press; teams that like to pressure the point guard will retreat, and the other team's center has to run with your post, creating fatigue.

The Designated Inbounder and Side Out-of-Bounds/ Baseline Out-of-Bounds Situations

The primary advantage of having a player who specializes in making the inbound pass in dead ball situations is the specific instruction the coach can give regarding all the possible scenarios in a basketball game. The coach can give this player the autonomy to make split-second decisions that can impact the outcome of a closely contested game, and the player will have the confidence necessary to make the correct decision.

The old adage that knowledge is power is often true when dealing with inbounders. Knowing what to do generates considerable confidence in what is often a pressure-filled situation.

Some of the tiny details the designated inbounder must know include:

- reading the positioning of the defense.
- passing away from the defense.
- passing away from the defender pressuring the ball.
- anticipating the actions of the defense as a unit.
- anticipating the actions of individuals on defense.
- when to call a time-out .
- communicating with officials in a positive manner.
- taking advantage of mismatches.
- knowing all the obscure rules that can impact an inbounds situation.

Chapter Ten

Character Counts

Great Teammates Inspire Confidence That the Team Can Succeed When Faced With Adversity

Every team will face adversity. It will come in every practice, every game, and every season. The great players are the ones who inspire their teammates, assuring them not only that everything will turn out fine but that each player is capable of handling adverse situations.

A classic example of this character and leadership was demonstrated by a former player of mine named Sam Coates. His team was down by nineteen on the road in a pivotal district game. During the break between the third and fourth periods, following my instructions to his teammates, Coates held his own coaching session. Fighting a fever and flu, he told his teammates, "Just play defense, funnel the ball to me, and we'll get the ball back. Then get me the ball and get out of my way. We're going to win this game."

I will never forget those words or the chill they sent down my spine. Coates proceeded to block nine shots, grab fourteen rebounds, and score twenty-nine unanswered points, leading his team to a dramatic victory. The opponent never scored in the fourth period, and Coates scored all but two of our points.

While Coates was certainly the focal point, his teammates truly played intense defense, forcing turnovers and funneling penetration to him. At six feet, seven inches, he was an excellent shot blocker. On offense Coates not only received the ball but also received it in his favorite scoring areas after being freed by solid screens.

To the average fan, it may have looked like the fourth quarter was all Sam Coates's, and make no mistake: without his herculean efforts, victory would not have been possible. But to the knowledgeable observer, it was obvious the dramatic win truly was a team effort. Without his teammates' increased effort and outstanding execution, Coates never would have been able to put on the heroic display of both offense and defense.

In talking to the players after the game, it became readily apparent that they truly believed when Coates issued his orders, a sleeping giant had awakened and was about to lead them to victory if only they would increase their efforts.

Why was Coates able to inspire such confidence in his them? Part of the answer lay in the fact that he was a tremendously skilled player and had demonstrated his prowess time after time in both practice and games. Coates also treated his teammates well over the course of his career. He always shared the credit, worked hard in practice and played even harder in games. He led by example and never asked his teammates to do something he was unwilling to do. He was physically and mentally tough and played that way every time he set foot on the floor. Coates took responsibility for the team's failures and willingly shared the praise for the team's success.

His teammates believed in his ability and his determination, and respected his leadership—a privilege Coates had earned. When he issued a call to step up and said they would overcome, they believed him, and they did not want to let him down. Thus they raised their own levels of mental and physical toughness, doubled their efforts, and worked to execute with just a little bit more precision.

Teams With Great Team Character Impose Their Will on Their Opponent on Key Possessions

A team's ability to impose its collective will on the opponent is key to success in an individual game and the entire season. A team that wants to play at a slow tempo must be able to impose that pace on an opponent that wants to fast break and play at a quick tempo. The team that can impose its will on the other will almost always win.

Imposing collective will on another group is not an easy task. It is truly a competition, not just between the two teams but also between the individuals who make up the teams. If one individual subjugates the team's will in order to achieve his personal goals, that can spell doom for the team's efforts in the struggle of wills.

Teams with great team character do not have issues with individual wills interfering. The individuals have already made the choice to humble themselves and submit their wills to that of the team, for the benefit of both the team and the individual.

Subjugating the individual will to the team does not mean the player loses his individuality. Rather it means he pledges his skills to the team. In doing so he can experience more personal success than when playing as an individual.

The nature of team play is truly a paradox in this sense. By submitting to the collective will of the team, the individual becomes more in the process.

Adversity and Competition Do Not Build Character— They Reveal It

One of the great myths about competition is that it builds character. Experience has shown it actually reveals an individual's character. Does the individual respond in a positive manner to adversity or the pressure of competition? Or does he crack? Does he respond to aggressive, dirty play in kind or play with sportsmanship at all times?

It does not take a lot of time and effort to conjure images of individuals who fit both of the aforementioned categories, and quite a few who fall somewhere in between the two extremes. So why do coaches, and society at large, continue to perpetuate the myth that competition builds character? The answer is that once character flaws are revealed, if the individual is mature enough to accept that he has a flaw, something can be done to rectify it.

The essential aspect of this process is that the individual has the humility to recognize and accept the flaw exists. Only when he takes ownership of a character trait can it be modified.

Those Who Suffer Most Surrender Last

Teams and individuals who have not invested in the process of challenging themselves and improving will give up at the first sign of adversity. Those who have paid a high price in the process of preparation and working to improve often relish the challenge of adversity and competition.

Not only do they tend to perform better, but due to the investments of time, effort, and energy, these teams and individuals will resist and compete until time runs out. They have invested too much to do otherwise.

Good Players Can Handle Criticism—Great Players Do Something About It

Nobody likes to be criticized. Usually it is not a pleasant experience. Most individuals reject any criticism of their play, ability, effort, and attitude.

However, good players can handle criticism. They do not demonstrate the typical negative reaction and negative body language everyone present can observe. This is certainly better than the typical response, but good players who can handle criticism are not taking advantage of what could potentially be a very helpful tool in their individual improvement.

Great players not only accept criticism; they embrace it if the critic is knowledgeable and fair. The critic's outside eyes can see flaws the great player cannot. By accepting criticism, the great player takes ownership of the flaw. This simple but difficult act allows the great player to move forward and work to eliminate the flaw.

Know What Your Weaknesses Are, Then Play to Your Strengths

Smart players know what their weaknesses are. They are also fully aware that if their weaknesses can be exploited by the opponent, it will be to the detriment of their team. These players exert considerable effort to take advantage of their strengths and not allow the opponent to take advantage of their weaknesses.

Know What Your Weaknesses Are and Work to Turn Them Into Strengths

Most players do not like to admit they have weaknesses in their game. Smart players take ownership of their weaknesses and work hard to eliminate them. Turning weaknesses into strengths one at a time is one of the best ways players can go from being just average to good or from good to great.

Players Must Take Ownership of Their Mistakes

Basketball is a game of mistakes. The team or player that can eliminate the greatest number of mistakes during a game is more likely to win.

Eliminating mistakes starts with what is the most difficult part for some players: admitting they've made a mistake.

Nobody likes to do this. The problem is, if a player is unwilling to recognize he made a mistake, hw cannot work to correct it and eliminate it from his game.

A good player recognizes he has made a mistake, takes ownership of it, learns from it, lets go of the memory, and moves on.

The Hardest Thing for People and Players to Do Is Serve Others

Basketball is a team sport. To play at a high level successfully, players must unite as a team. Being part of a team requires that they serve each other. This could be as simple as setting a screen for another player, giving help on defense, or penetrating to create a shot for another player. It could be as complex and difficult as helping a teammate who has a personal problem.

It's human nature for individuals to think of themselves first and foremost. Serving others is a learned behavior, and it is not easy to learn for most individuals.

Thinking Only of Yourself and What You Want Will Make You Miserable

Individuals who show no concern for others and think only of themselves are destined for misery. Human happiness is meant to be shared and often comes only when successful interaction has taken place.

The most joyous events in an individual's life almost always require others' presence—for example weddings, the birth of a child, or a team winning a championship. For these events to be truly joyful, all of the individuals involved must make a concerted effort to think about the wants and needs of the others involved. Part of the joy is in the simple act of sharing the experience with another human being.

When individuals think only of themselves, they deny themselves the greatest source of joy: sharing with others.

Mentally Tough Players Play Through Adversity

Adversity strikes in every game. The average player often allows this to become an emotional issue and focuses on the unfairness of the adverse situation, such as a poor call or no call by an official. By focusing on the adverse situation, the player is no longer in control.

Mentally tough players are aware that an adverse situation has taken place. They simply move on and focus on what they have control over, and continue to play in the moment, focusing on the game at that instant instead of wallowing in the emotional turmoil of adversity.

Never put your hands on your knees. It signals to you and your opponent that you are either physically or mentally tired, or both.

Humility Is a Sign of Greatness

Great players are aware their success is dependent on the efforts of their teammates. Humility allows a great player to recognize this fact and to recognize publicly his teammates' contributions to his success.

The arrogance of a single player can quickly divide a team. Players understandably resent one teammate's refusal to recognize the contributions all the individual players make so the group and the other individual players can succeed.

It takes a mature player to step aside and let others have the spotlight so the team and the other players can succeed.

Chapter Eleven
Rebounding

Don't Get Rebounds—Grab Them

This may seem like a subtle concept, but it is not. Rebounding is an aggressive activity requiring an aggressive attitude or mentality. Getting a rebound is more passive than grabbing one. If an individual is told to go and get an object, there is a lot of implied latitude in how the individual can go about obtaining the object. Telling an individual to grab an object implies a degree of aggressiveness that the word *get* does not. The visual image of grabbing an object is of someone reaching out and aggressively snatching it, then quickly gathering it to their body.

Grab Every Rebound

Great rebounders all respond the same when asked what the key is to grabbing as many rebounds as they did during a game. The answer is always simple but not easy to accomplish: they did not try to get ten or twelve rebounds in a game; they tried to grab every single rebound, and they did so with a relentlessness that bordered on obsession.

The logic is simple. If they only tried to grab ten or twelve rebounds a game, their opponent would be able to stop them about two thirds of the time, if not more. But if they relentlessly tried to obtain the rebound from every single missed shot in the game, even if they only obtained one third of the misses they would dominate the boards and be a major factor in helping their team win the game.

Use Both Hands With Fingers on the Top Half of the Ball

One of the worst habits a player can develop is using one hand to obtain a rebound. The only time this technique is acceptable is when it is not possible to grab the rebound with both hands. The reason is simple: using one hand provides less control over the ball than using two does.

The player should grab the rebound with both hands and establish control of the ball with his fingers on the top half of the ball. This method provides the player with the greatest amount of control of the ball—an essential factor when rebounding in traffic.

Chin the Ball

Once a player has grabbed a rebound with both hands, with the fingers on the top half of the ball, he must safely secure it from the opposition, who will attempt to strip or otherwise knock it lose. The only acceptable method is to rip the ball aggressively downward and secure it with both hands underneath the chin, with both elbows sticking out.

This technique places the ball in the most protected position the player can hold it in. All basketball players can hold the ball with the greatest amount of strength they're capable of when the ball is chinned. An opponent can strike the ball with considerable force and it will not be dislodged.

Believe Every Shot Will Be Missed

Great rebounders believe every shot will be missed, and their goal is to grab every rebound from a missed shot. This mindset helps them to have an aggressive outlook about rebounding, gaining position, and pursuing the ball when the shot is missed.

Anticipate Where the Ball Will Come Off the Goal

Half of the battle to grab a rebound is getting to the ball before another player does. Hockey great Wayne Gretzky was once asked why he was always in the right place at the right time to score goals. His response was he looked for where the shot would be open and then skated to that spot. Rebounders should have the same mindset. When a shot is taken, the rebounder should anticipate where the rebound will come off the goal and go to that spot.

Equal Opposite Angle

I learned this concept from my high school geometry teacher, and it served me well as a player. Missed shots usually rebound from the goal at an angle roughly equal and opposite to the angle at which the ball hit the goal. This does not hold true with every missed shot, but it does apply for most. Using this concept a player can estimate where the ball will go if the shot is missed, and begin to move toward where the rebound will be instead of waiting until the ball impacts the goal and comes off as a miss.

Half the Distance

Another useful concept in estimating where a rebound will go is that missed shots travel out from the goal roughly half the distance of where the shot was taken from. Shots taken from six to eight feet will come out three to four feet from the goal. Shots taken from behind the three-point line will rebound a much greater distance—often as far as ten to twelve feet—and sometimes are more like loose balls than rebounds. Again, using this concept with the concept of the equal opposite angle will give an advantage to the cunning player who anticipates.

Tip to Control—Short Post

The only time it is acceptable to use one hand to rebound is when it is not possible to grab the rebound. In order to prevent the opponent from grabbing of the ball, tip it away from him and toward the short post area on the baseline. Once the ball has successfully been tipped to this area, the rebounder has an advantage since he knows where the ball is going, and he can quickly pursue it and obtain possession of it for his team.

Offensive Rebounds May Be More Important

Offensive rebounds may be more important than defensive rebounds. If a team can obtain one third of the offensive shots missed, they can obtain a significant statistical advantage in the total number of shots taken.

The logic behind this concept is that the team that takes the greatest number of shots will have a greater chance of scoring more points. Since the object of the game of basketball is to outscore the opponent, teams should do everything possible to increase the total number of shots taken in a game.

This strategy requires forcing the opponent into a large number of turnovers *and* grabbing as rebounds a high percentage of offensive field goal attempts that are missed. Obtaining one third of all missed field goal attempts is the same as having one third more possessions than the opponent.

Point Guards Should Lead the Team in Defensive Rebounding

Since most teams send the offensive point guard to half court to begin the floor balance phase of defensive transition, the defensive point guard has no practical responsibility to block out an offensive player and is free to anticipate where the rebound will come off the goal, and to pursue and grab the ball.

Coaches must emphasize the point guards' freedom to rebound on defense and emphasize the opportunity to grab rebounds. In fact they should insist point guards grab rebounds when on the defensive end of the court.

You Can Be as Selfish As You Want As a Rebounder

Rebounding is the one statistical area in the game of basketball where selfishness can be tolerated. No coach will ever tell a player to let a teammate grab a rebound. The only danger in this scenario is that the other players will come to rely on the outstanding rebounder and stop attempting to grab rebounds.

Know Your Arena

Every arena is different. Every goal is different. The differences will impact how a ball will come off the rim or backboard when a shot is missed. Rims that are mounted more tightly or without the pad behind the rim will produce a longer rebound on a miss. Goals that are mounted rigidly on a wall will also tend to produce somewhat longer rebounds on missed shots.

Rims that are loose or bent will have shorter rebounds that come off at unusual angles. The good rebounder factors these subtle differences in when determining where the rebound will come off the goal.

Box In Instead of Out When a Three-Point Shot Has Been Taken

This concept may seem counterintuitive given the time and effort coaches expend teaching players to box out in order to obtain a rebound. Since missed three-point shots yield longer rebounds, it is to the aggressive rebounder's advantage to have an outside position instead of an inside position when a three-point field goal is attempted. By pinning the opponent in instead of boxing them out, the aggressive rebounder is in a better position to pursue and grab the long rebound.

Play With Your Hands Up

Jumping is a bit overrated in rebounding. Desire, position, hustle, and upper body strength are more important. The player who can get and maintain arm dominance (having his arms and hands over the opponent's) will have a much greater chance to grab the rebound.

Watch films of the great rebounders and you will see this is true. Bill Walton would run down the court with his hands up and always fought to have arm dominance. Dennis Rodman would fight to keep his arms free. Having his hands up higher than the opponent's gives a player a greater chance to grab the rebound first simply because his hands are closer to the ball.

Jump Like a Jet, Not Like a Rocket

Rebounders must go and grab the ball. Rebounders who wait for the ball to come to them will not be very successful. Players must jump to where the ball will be, not just straight up in the air, hoping the ball comes to them. Picture a rocket taking off: it goes straight up and is fairly slow in comparison to a jet. Now picture a jet. It goes up at an angle and with much greater velocity. The rebounder who has more velocity and jumps to where the ball will be will get the rebound almost every time.

BOPCRO

Coach Don Meyer developed this acronym, and it is excellent for players to adopt as part of their mindset. It stands for: **B**lock **O**ut, **P**ursue the ball, **C**hin the ball, **R**ebound, and **O**utlet pass.

Chapter Twelve

Shooting

The Most Important Shooting Coach a Player Can Have Is Himself

Players benefit from instruction from coaches who can expertly teach skills, particularly how to shoot a basketball. During a game a player does not have the benefit of having a coach observe his shot repeatedly to find the flaw that causes him to miss.

For this reason the player must understand how to correct flaws in his own shot. He must have enough technical knowledge about shooting and the knowledge of how his own shot feels kinesthetically when performed correctly. This allows the player to recognize what is wrong with his shot and correct it during a game.

Hold a High, One-Second Follow-Through After Shooting

There is more than one correct way to shoot a basketball, and some methods are better than others. Even if two players are both taught to shoot with the best method, there will be slight differences in the mechanics of their shots.

Regardless of what a player has learned, most of the great shooters all hold a high, one-second follow-through after shooting the ball. A high follow-through is when the player's shooting elbow is above his eyebrow. He must hold that position or pose for one second with a proper follow-through. The last finger to leave the ball should be in line with the shooter's target.

The high follow-through ensures the shot will be close to the desired sixty-degree arc while in flight. The follow-through ensures the ball will have the desired backspin, which increases the likelihood the shot will go in if it should impact on the rim.

If You Must Miss a Shot, Miss It Long or Short, But Not Left or Right

If a player misses a shot, it should be long or short and not left and right. A player should always strive to keep his shot line straight. This is an easy repair to make—the player can simply follow through with a little less force to shorten the shot or a little more force for to lengthen it.

Shots that are missed to the left or right can mean a myriad of issues in the shooting technique, such as the player's not squaring up properly or pushing the ball with the balance hand. These can be difficult to address.

The primary reason a player wants to make certain he misses long or short but not left or right is shooter's roll. A shot that is too long or too short but has the correct amount of backspin and is at a sixty-degree arc will bounce more or less straight up in the area over the rim. A good percentage of these misses will go in. Shots missed to the left or right will bounce away from the goal after impact.

A Basketball Player Must Warm Up His Shot

Shooters, like pitchers in baseball warming up their arms before taking the field, must warm up their shots. Too many players walk into a gym, pick up a basketball, and start shooting three-point shots immediately. The good and great shooters warm up their shots.

To warm up a shot properly, a player needs a set routine that emphasizes muscle memory and correct technique. Another essential element is for the player to start shooting two feet from the goal and then slowly working out to his maximum shooting range.

When players use this approach, they are much more consistent, and their field goal percentages are higher. The key element is the process of starting in close for the first shots and then working out to the edge of the shooter's range. This concept is key because the player has immediate success in terms of making shots. Nothing boosts a shooter's confidence like seeing the ball go through the rim and swishing the net!

When a Player Has a Flaw in His Shot, Correct It by Working on the Free-Throw Shot

The basic mechanics of the jump shot, power shot, or three-point shot are those of the free throw. When a player has a flaw in his shot, the best way to work to correct it, according to none other than Coach Don Meyer, is for the player to shoot free throws from the foul line. This approach makes good sense, as the shot is the same every time and is from the same exact location. The consistency in distance and location allows the player to make basic judgments about what is wrong with the shot or how it feels.

Point the Toes at the Baseline When Shooting a Power Shot Inside

Players are taught to square up to shoot, and for nearly every shot having the shoulders square to the rim or target is the correct technique. As with many rules, there is an exception to this one.

If a player squares up to shoot a short-range power shot using the backboard, the shot will most likely be blocked and no foul will be called. The reason for this is the shooter will show his numbers to the interior defender, giving him an excellent look at the ball and time to block.

If the shooter points his toes at the baseline, the angle of his body in relationship to the defender changes dramatically. His shoulder is between the defender and the ball. The shooter must reach across the inside shoulder and arm of the shooter to block or contest a shot. This looks like a foul—and usually is.

To maximize the impact of this adjustment, the wise shooter will try to position his inside shoulder—the one closest to the middle of the lane—just under the net. This seals the defensive player in such a poor position, the only way to contest the shot is to foul or interfere with the net, resulting in a goaltending violation.

When Shooting a Bank Shot, Kiss the Ball off the Glass High and Soft

The object in using the backboard when shooting is to shoot the highest possible field goal percentage. To obtain the maximum positive effect of using the backboard, the shooter must shoot the ball at such an angle that it strikes the backboard at or above the top of the square marked or shooters to use as a target. The shooter also wants to have the ball impact the glass as softly as possible. A soft impact does not alter the angle of rebound off the glass, ensuring the ball travels along the shot line the shooter intended.

Players commonly make two errors, or a combination of them, when using the backboard. The first is to shoot a line drive shot off the backboard. Players do make field goal attempts shooting like this, but the shot must impact the backboard in a single precise spot. Any deviation from the precise angle will result in a miss.

The other common mistake is to shoot the ball at such a low angle it impacts the backboard at a poor angle, or so low it cannot go through the rim.

Players are often guilty of shooting the ball too low and too hard. The higher up on the backboard it impacts, the less precise the angle of impact must be. The greater the variation of acceptable error in the shot, the greater the chance the ball will go through the rim. Kissing the ball off the glass gives the shooter the greatest chance for bounce, again increasing the chance the ball will enter the rim for a goal.

The Worst Shot in the Game of Basketball

This is when a player stands with one foot, or part of a foot, on the three-point line when shooting. This shot is only worth two points if it is made, and it is the poorest-percentage two-point shot that can be taken. Simply moving back far enough to make certain both feet are behind the three-point line makes the shot good. The value of the made attempt is three points instead of two.

The percentages of shooting come into play in this example. A good field goal percentage for a two-point shooter is forty five to fifty percent. A good field goal percentage for a three-point shooter is thirty-three percent. If a shooter takes one hundred two-point field goal attempts and makes fifty percent of them, he will score one hundred points. If the same shooter takes one hundred three-point shots and makes thirty-three percent, he will score ninety-nine points.

A two-point shot attempt that a shooter will make on average only thirty-three percent of the time is a poor shot. A three-point shot rewards the shooter with an extra point when the shot is made even though the field goal percentage for a shot taken from roughly the same distance is still only thirty-three percent.

If a player is going to take a thirty-three percent shot, it needs to be worth three points. If it's not, over the course of the game or a season, the additional missed shots will haunt that player's team because when the shot is made, the reward is only two points.

A Jump Shooter Should Land Just Slightly Forward in His Own Footprints

Shooters do not want to drift when shooting a jump shot. Drifting to the left, right, front, or rear decreases the shooter's accuracy and increases the potential for mechanical errors to creep into the shot. For example a right-handed jump shooter's drifting to the right on a jump shot will tend to cause the shooter to turn his body into the shot toward the left, pushing the shot line of the ball to the left, causing the shot to be missed to the left.

A good tool for shooters to use to prevent drifting is the two-inch rule, in which the shooter lowers his rear two inches in the triple threat when stopping, then raises two inches again. This simple skill directs all of the directional momentum, which can cause a shooter to drift in one direction or another, eliminating it as a problem.

Another good tool for shooters to prevent drifting is landing in their own footprints, or just slightly forward if necessary. A shooter does want to land just slightly the forward; the slight forward momentum of his body helps both to propel the ball forward to the goal and to align the shot with the goal. By attempting to land in his own footprints, a player will naturally land just slightly forward but still in alignment with his original takeoff point. Telling players they have permission to land just slightly forward of their footprints prevents them from overcorrecting and, in doing so, causing technique problems.

Forget the Fade Away Shot

The fade away looks pretty—when it goes in, that is. Some players can shoot the fade away with great success. They are gifted shooters who have perfected their basic shooting techniques. Given a choice, they will always choose a shot that allows them to square up, get an unobstructed look at their target, and shoot on balance. Before a player starts spending hours on perfecting his fade away shot, he should perfect his basic shot.

Sight a Specific Target When Shooting—the More Specific the Better

The human brain is in many ways like a targeting computer in an ICBM: the more specific the information the targeting computer receives, the more accurate the missile strike will be. The more specific a target a shooter has, the more accurately the brain will target the shot.

Players who have excellent mechanics but are poor shooters, when asked what they aim at or what target they sight, will often respond that they look at the entire goal. Great shooters have very specific targets. It could be the one inch of rim opposite where he is shooting, or it could be two inches above the dead center of the rim. Regardless, the key is the shooter must have a very specific target.

A note about targets: Shooters who target the area just behind the front of the rim miss a high percentage of shots by shooting short. The brain has the ball travel exactly where the shooter aims, but most shots fall just a little short. Thus the shooters who use this area tend to shoot short.

Backspin Is What Allows Misses to Go In

Have a player take a basketball and toss it with no backspin so it bounces on the court. When the ball impacts it will develop a slight frontspin, causing it to move in the direction opposite the player who tossed the ball. Now have a player take a basketball and toss it with backspin. Now when the ball impacts the court, the backspin stops and the ball bounces straight up with no spin at all, falling just an inch or two behind the initial contact point.

This phenomenon is what creates shooter's roll. A shot with no backspin or with frontspin will not go through the rim when the shot is off just enough for the ball to impact the top of the rim, creating a miss. A ball with backspin that impacts the top of the rim will bounce straight up and remain in the area over the rim, allowing some chance that the ball will pass through the rim when it descends.

Chapter Thirteen

Fine Tuning the Fast Break

Fundamentals Are Essential, and Players Must Be Able to Execute Them Perfectly at Game Speed

Fundamentals are key in any phase of the game for a player and a team to be successful. This is especially true for the fast break phase. The speed involved magnifies the positive and negative aspects of the game.

Just as the fast break will yield open shots, clear driving lanes to the goal, and the ability to score large amounts of points in a short period, so does the opportunity to make bad passes, travel, or mishandle a ball. Players and coaches must understand this aspect of fast-break basketball.

The key to maximizing the positive aspects while negating or reducing the negative is to mast the fundamentals at game speed. This means the fundamentals must be practiced and per-fected at the same rapid pace at which fast-break basketball is played during a game.

The Best Ball Handler/Decision Maker Handles the Ball

Too often a scoring opportunity is lost following an oppo-nent's turnover because the defender who secured possession of the ball tries to bring the ball up himself. This is not a problem if the player is a good ball handler, a good passer on the run, and a good finisher at the goal.

The smartest play is always to get the ball to the best handler available and allow that individual to run the fast break. This ensures the greatest number of fast break opportunities will be converted into points for the fast break team.

If the best ball handler is a poor decision maker, the ball should be given to the player who is the best decision maker and still has reasonable ball handling skills.

Pass for a Score

The ball handler/decision maker who leads the fast break should think in terms of one pass, and that pass should be for a scoring opportunity. The more passes the attacking fast break team has to make in order to score, the greater the chance the opponent will be able to recover and establish defensive resistance.

Get the Ball to the Best Finisher/Shooter

The ball handler/decision maker must use the concept of *best* in his decision making process. The ideal pass for a score pass is to the best finisher or shooter, giving the offense the best chance to score on the fast break opportunity.

Too often the ball handler/decision maker passes to a good offensive player who is not good at scoring on the run in a fast-break situation. Take the Showtime Lakers of the 1980s for example. You would never see Magic passing to Kareem on the dead run to finish the fast break. Magic was looking for James Worthy, Michael Cooper, or Byron Scott. Kareem was a fantastic offensive player, but his strength as a scorer was operating from the offensive low post with his back to the basket, not filling a fast-break lane. Worthy was a great finisher on the break, and as such a much better target for Magic when the Lakers were running.

Make the Easy Pass, Not the Assist Pass

Critics of fast-break basketball believe the running game results in too many turnovers. One of the best safeguards against turning the ball over in any style of offensive play is for coaches to emphasize making the easy pass and not the fancy assist pass.

This is a concept that bears coaches repeating it on a daily basis. Even if the passer is capable of a great-thread-the needle pass, is the receiver capable of catching it? The passer should always look for the easiest pass that can be made, and then the pass must be made away from the defense, with zip and right to the target.

Always Run at Warp Speed

Lots of teams, players, and coaches say they want to play fast-break basketball, but when it is time for the rubber to meet the road, they are not committed. Like many things in life, you cannot do this halfway. Either play a controlled tempo or play a fast-tempo style. If the decision is made to try to do both, then both will suffer. If the decision has been made to run and play fast, then play fast. Run at warp speed every time possession of the ball is obtained.

If You are Going to Run, Run on Everything

Again the decision must be made to run or not run. Once the decision to play up-tempo has been made, and the players have been trained to run at warp speed on every possession, the next element is to learn to run on every possession.

This means teams run off dead balls, jump balls, turnovers, defensive rebounds, and made baskets. There is no situation a team cannot fast-break attack from except possibly an inbounds from underneath its own basket.

When Filling the Lane, Get Wide First

Players, in their excitement over a fast-break scoring opportunity, often sprint as hard as they can up the court. Their effort and desire to fill a fast-break lane and score is commendable. But all too often they simply run in a straight line from the spot they were in when possession of the ball was obtained.

Filling the so-called fast-break lanes in this manner fails to accomplish two essential elements for the fast break to score consistently. The first is to obtain good passing and attack angles for scoring. The second is to spread the defenders out as much as possible, to create open lanes of attack and viable passing lanes.

In order to build the habit of getting wide, players must be taught to do so first and then run the fast-break lane. This begs the question: what is wide enough? Former Lakers Coach Pat Riley taught his players to step out of bounds at the half-court line to ensure they ran their fast-break lanes wide enough.

Never Deviate From the Pattern

If a team runs a highly controlled numbered break in which specific players fill specific fast-break lanes and run to specific spots on the floor, they must never be allowed to deviate from that pattern in practice, and as much as possible in games.

Give the players one thing to do. Have them do it at maximum speed and with perfect fundamentals every single time. The opponent might know exactly what the offense wants to do, but by perfecting the running system, whatever the system might be, the offense can make it into a contest of wills. The team whose will prevails should win the game. Fast-break basketball, in many ways, is not finesse basketball but rather sledgehammer basketball.

A Turnover Means the Team Did Not Get to Shoot the Ball

Critics of fast-break basketball like to point at the high number of turnovers fast-break teams commit as a reason not to play an up-tempo style. No coach should tolerate turnovers for one simple reason: a turnover means the team did not get an opportunity to shoot before relinquishing control of the ball.

Regardless of the tempo or style of basketball, players must be taught to value possession of the ball. A team cannot score without first possessing the ball. It is that simple.

The Inbounds Pass Is the Key to Running Off a Made Basket

There are several equally successful and viable tactics to inbounds the ball in this situation. The one key factor is not the tactic used but rather having a designated inbounder who can get the ball out of the net and into the hands of the point guard in 1.5 seconds or less following every made basket.

The Second Pass Is the Key Pass

The pass following the initial outlet pass is the key to the success of the break. Some teams like to advance the ball up the court with a long pass to one of the wings filling a lane. Other teams like to advance the ball by pushing it rapidly up the floor on the dribble, using as few dribbles as possible.

If the ball is to be advanced up the court by passing rather than dribbling, the key is how quickly it is passed across half court, catching the defenders on the open floor while in transition.

If the ball is to be advanced up the court by dribbling with as few dribbles as possible, the second pass must be for a score if at all possible.

Dribble As Little As Possible

Fast is the key descriptive word in the phrase *fast break*. You never hear anyone refer to a *slow break*. Speed is the essential element. The more the ball handler/decision maker dribbles, the slower the ball is advanced up the floor. A good ball handler/decision maker can push the ball up the floor from outlet to rim in four dribbles.

Less Is More

Coaches love to tinker with their offensive and defensive systems. They love to add plays and new defenses. In the case of the fast break, coaches love to add new secondary breaks or special little twists for the players to run.

The more the players have to remember, the more they have to think. The more they have to think, the less they can act instinctively based on the good habits that have been instilled in them by good coaching.

The less players have to remember, the less they have to think. The less they have to think, the more they can act instinctively on the good habits that have been instilled in them by good coaching.

Good coaches believe less is more. The less the players have to think, the more the players can do. If he does have to add something to the offense, the defense, or the fast break, a good coach takes something out of the system so the players do not have more to remember.

Run Lanes to Perfection Each Time

Regardless of the fast-break system that is taught, players must run their lanes to perfection each time. They cannot choose which possessions they will run to perfection on and which they will coast on. Each possession is valuable, and each must be taken advantage of. Players must understand it's not the shot missed at the buzzer that loses them the close game—it's the one possession they did not run to perfection.

The Harder You Run, the Longer You Have to Shoot

The faster a player runs his fast-break lane, the more pressure the defense is under to make a transition into the lane. The faster the offensive player is able to get to his spot on the floor in a fast break, the greater the period between the arrival of the defense and the reception of the pass for a score.

Sound defense begins from the inside out. Defensive players are trained to make transitions to the lanes and defend the rim first, then close out on the perimeter players and establish the set five-on-five defense with ball side and help side. This entire process takes a few seconds even when the defensive team is well organized and disciplined, and hustles on each defensive possession.

The sooner the offensive player is able to reach his spot on the floor in transition, the more time during the period of defensive transition he will have to shoot the ball, allowing for an open, unhurried shot. In other words the harder you run, the longer you have to shoot.

Players Must Play So Hard Their Feet and Lungs Burn

Players must play hard regardless of style of play. Those who play on a fast-breaking team must play harder than members of teams that play at a slower tempo. Players often want to know just how hard they have to play. The answer is simple: players must play so hard their lungs feel like they are burning and their feet feel like they are on fire.

Conditioning Is Paramount

Fast-break offense teams must be in excellent condition. Not only must the players be able to have excellent endurance, but they must be able to accelerate and decelerate quickly, and have excellent agility. The ability to repeat explosive movements such as jumping and accelerating quickly over and over is also essential. Poorly conditioned athletes in a fast-break system are doomed to fail.

A Fast-Break Team Must Be More Disciplined than a Deliberate Team

Many individuals believe fast-break basketball lacks discipline. Nothing is further from the truth when it comes to good fast-break teams.

The first area of discipline that must be instilled in a fast-break team's players is the ability to push beyond fatigue. The average players will slow down when fatigue becomes a factor. Fast-break teams must play through the fatigue and take advantage of the fatigue the other team is experiencing.

Possession of the ball is another aspect of discipline fast-break teams must develop. Each possession of the ball is valuable. A turnover means individual possession resulted in a loss of a shot attempt. It also means an opportunity to press and maintain tempo might have been lost as well. Good fast-break teams average the same number of actual turnovers that good, disciplined, deliberate half-court teams average. What is deceiving about this stat is the fast-break team is actually better at taking care of the possession of the ball than the deliberate team.

If both teams have twelve turnovers for a game, the fast-break team takes better care of its possessions of the ball. Because of the tempo it creates, it will have a significantly higher number of possessions than the deliberate team. An identical number of turnovers by the two teams means the fast-break team actually has the lowest percentage of turnovers out of the total number of possessions.

Defense Is What Speeds the Game Up, Not Offense

Most people think a fast-break offense is what speeds up the tempo of a game. It is not. Deliberate teams that are disciplined simply take their normal amount of time to work for a good shot opportunity, and sometimes will even pass up the first good shot opportunity to lengthen the time of the possession. This can prevent a fast-break team from speeding up the pace of the game.

Pressure defense that forces offensive action on the part of the other team, combined with the fast-break offensive attack, is what speeds up the tempo of the game.

Cut in Straight Lines When Attacking the Basket

When cutting to the basket to attack, wings often make a banana-shaped cut instead of a straight line. The curved cut moves the cutter toward the baseline and decreases the angle to the goal. This slight angle creates a very difficult shot.

The player who uses straight lines and sharp angles when attacking the goal from the wings during the fast break will have an excellent forty-five-degree angle at which to shoot a layup. Utilizing proper angles and cuts is a major part of fulfilling the concept of running the break to perfection.

Players Must Be Able to Read the Defense and Make Sound Decisions

It is not the obvious defender who often steals the ball or intercepts the pass; it is the help-side defender lurking, anticipating, and waiting for the pass to be made. It is not the defender who appears to be ready to attack who intercepts the pass; it is the one who looks relaxed but whose body weight is leaning in the direction of the anticipated pass.

Good passers on the fast break must be able to read not only the floor location of the defenders but their body language as well. This skill by itself can eliminate a large number of turnovers.

Teams Must Be Able to Score Every Time in a Two-on-One Situation

A team must convert every two-on-one situation into points or a trip to the foul line. The first element of successfully doing this is for the ball to be in the hands of the best ball handler/decision maker, and for the other offensive player in the two on one to get wide—which, in this situation, means both players are as wide as the three-point line at the free throw line extended area when moving into the attack area.

Simply by getting wide, the lone defender is forced to select between stopping the ball handler and defending the cutter. Regardless of which offensive player the defender selects, the other player should be able to shoot a layup.

A simple ball handling maneuver ensures one of the two offensive players will shoot a layup. As the ball handler/decision maker approaches the foul line extended area, he moves the ball to the hand on the side of the offensive cutter. This means if the ball handler/decision maker is on the right-hand side of the court and the cutter is on the left, the ball is moved to the left hand.

This simple ball handling maneuver allows the ball handler/decision maker to draw the defender to him and easily make a bounce pass to the cutter without having to bring the ball in front of the defender.

Turn All Three-on-One and Three-on-Two Situations Into Two-on-One Situations

While it's not quite as easy as a two-on-one fast break, coaches should expect their players to convert ninety to ninety-five percent of all three-on-one and three-on-two fast-break situations into points or a trip to the foul line. To obtain such a high rate, the players must convert the three-on-one and three-on-two situations into two-on-one situations. This is done by veering in one direction as the ball handler approaches the attack zone, with the two wings running their lanes as wide as possible.

The concept of *best* applies here. The best ball handler/decision maker will have the ball in the middle of the court. The ball handler/decision maker must read the defense and determine the best shot available for the three players involved in the fast break.

If one of the players is the team's best finisher, the ball handler/decision maker should veer away from him. In a three-on-one situation, this turns the play into a two-on-one and is executed in the same manner, including the location of the ball by the ball handler just prior to drawing the defender and making the pass for a score.

The same tactic is used in converting a three-on-two into a two-on-one. By veering away from the best finisher, the lead defender, who is responsible for stopping and pressuring the ball, is taken out of the passing lane between the ball handler/decision maker and the best finisher. For some reason the second defender, who must defend the cutter who receives the first pass, will cheat to the side of the court the ball handler/decision maker veers to. This shift by both players creates the desired two-on-one situation, allowing for the high-percentage conversion of the offensive play.

If the defense does not challenge the ball handler/decision maker, or the ball handler/decision maker is the best finisher, then the ball handler should attack and score.

Give the Cutter the Ball Where He Can Do Something With It

It makes no sense to pass the ball to the seven foot All-American post player who has no outside shot but is utterly dominating in the offensive low post—not until that player has successfully posted up and is ready to receive the ball. Nor does it make sense to pass the ball to the great, undersized three-point shooter when he has cut into the low post.

The ball should be passed to a player where he can have success once in possession of the ball. This means passing the ball to the great three-point shooter for a three-point shot. Pass the ball to the seven-foot center in the low post and pass the ball to the great finisher on the wing during the fast break.

This concept also applies to specific locations on the court. The great finisher needs enough room to dribble once, cut around a defender, or pull up for a jump shot. A pass that draws him too close to the goal does not afford him room to operate.

The great three-point shooter might not shoot particularly well from the corners but will knock three-point shots down all night from the wings and the top of the key. In this instance do not pass the ball to the great three-point shooter in the corner. It is not productive for the team or the player.

Cutters and Penetrators Must Be Able to Finish at the Rim

Because of the large amount of contact and limited space around the rim, players often have a difficult time scoring with a traditional running layup. To make sure all layup attempts result in points, a trip to the foul line, or, ideally, both points and a trip to the foul line, players must be taught how to shoot power layups. They are easy to execute out of a half-court offense but are more difficult following an all-out sprint up the court.

This is an example of why fundamental skills must be practiced and perfected at game speed and in conditions that are as game-like as possible.

The Ball Handler Should Step to the Corner of the Lane After Passing on the Break, Never Penetrating

In all primary break situations, if the ball handler makes a pass to a wing prior to penetrating the foul line, the passer should step quickly to the ball-side elbow, sometimes called the T, at the foul line in order to receive a possible pass back for a shot. If the ball handler is a great three-point shooter, he should step to a spot behind the three-point line but up the ball-side lane line, extended to receive a pass back.

Continuing into the lane after passing allows the defense to take a charge off the passer and only congests the lane for the cutter who has just received the pass.

If the Cutter Cannot Score, He Should Quick Stop and Euro the Ball Back to the Passer

If a cutter cannot score on the fast-break attack after receiving a pass, he should execute a jump stop directly in front of the defender who has eliminated the lane to the goal, execute a rear turn with the ball tight to his chest, and execute a Euro pass back to the passer who has stepped to the ball side for a return pass and a shot.

This tactic can also be used by the ball handler if he has penetrated the lane. In this example the wing on the side of the penetrated lane would quickly cut to a spot behind the ball handler, often for a three-point attempt.

Teach Shot Selection

Shooting is not an equal-opportunity skill, nor should it be. The best shooters should take the bulk of the shots. This does not mean players who are not particularly good shooters should never shoot.

What this does mean is coaches must teach good shot selection. What is a good shot for one player is not a good shot for another player. What was a good shot for one player early in the game might not be good for the same player later in the game, all depending on the time and score when the second shot opportunity presents itself.

Chapter Fourteen

Control

Control What You Can

Basketball can sometimes be describe as somewhat controlled chaos, and the team that is able to bring the most order has the best chance of winning the game. This might be overstating things a bit, but at times it certainly seems like an accurate statement. What is certain is there are many elements over which both a coach and players have no control.

No coach is able to control how tall the opponent's center is, how quick the opponent's point guard is, or the range of the opponent's shooters. Nor can any player control an official's calls, the physical condition of the court and building the game is played in, or the speed of the clock.

In fact there are really only three things a coach and a player have control over. God gave each individual total control over the choices he makes, his attitude, and his effort. Nothing else can be controlled by an individual. It is a waste of time and emotional and mental energy to try. In fact it can result in a great deal of negative behavior, thinking, actions, and mistakes on the court.

One of the traits of a good team is that the players are able to accept adversity, which comes in every game and every season, and not only deal with it but thrive because or in spite of it. Such a team chooses to deal with adversity in a positive, constructive manner. In other words the team chooses to have a positive attitude about the situation, and realizes the only control they have over it at the moment is to move forward and not allow any negativity to impact their effort. They choose to play through the adversity. This approach often results in a positive outcome for the team; they turn the adverse situation into an advantage.

For a team to adopt this view requires a coach who models it for them. It requires that the coach invest a great deal of time and effort in teaching it to each player, and the players in turn will transform this view into an action by displaying this attitude through their actions.

Too many times coaches and players get caught up in a mistake, an adverse situation, or something that causes adversity, and, by not letting go of it and moving on, cause considerable negative impact for the individuals and thus for the team. This sort of thing manifests in many negative ways: improper or unsportsmanlike behavior, a technical foul, becoming so upset emotionally or rattled mentally that performance is negatively impacted, etc. The list of possibilities is quite long.

What players and coaches can do when something adverse happens is take ownership, learn from it, and move on. It sounds simple, but it is not. It takes a great deal of mental discipline, but it can be learned.

What a coach can do proactively, in the mold of controlling what can be controlled, is prepare his team for any adverse situations they might face during the season or a game. This requires considerable planning on a coach's part, and it is the purpose of this small book to help.

Players are much more likely to handle adversity successfully if they are prepared for it and know what to do. It's like peer pressure: it's easy to make the right choice if you've already decided, before you are confronted with the choice. Players and teams are more likely to make the correct choices when they have already rehearsed the proper responses to the adverse situations.

Chapter Fifteen
There Is More to Learn

Suggested Reading List
Practical Modern Basketball by John Wooden
Game Strategy and Tactics for Basketball: Bench Coaching for Success by Kevin Sivils
Wooden: A Lifetime of Observations and Reflections On and Off the Court by John Wooden with Steve Jamison
They Call Me Coach by John Wooden
Coach Wooden One-on-One by John Wooden and Jay Carty
Wooden on Leadership by John Wooden
Coach Wooden's Pyramid of Success Playbook by John Wooden and Jay Carty
John Wooden's UCLA Offense by John Wooden and Sven Nader
You Haven't Taught Until They Have Learned: John Wooden's Teaching Principles and Practices by Sven Nader, Ronald Gallimore, and Bill Walton
They Call Me Coach by John Wooden
Basketball: Multiple Offense and Defense by Dean Smith
Basketball: Skills & Drills by Jerry Krause, Don Meyer, and Jerry Meyer
Basketball Skill Progressions by Jerry Krause
Don Meyer's Coaching Academy Notebooks 1998–2007

The Lipscomb Program by Don Meyer

Basketball According to Knight and Newell, Volume I by Bob Knight and Pete Newell

Basketball According to Knight and Newell, Volume II by Bob Knight and Pete Newell

Coaching Basketball Successfully by Morgan Wootten With Dave Gilbert

The Seven Secrets of Successful Coaches: How to Unlock and Unleash Your Team's Full Potential by Jeff Janssen, MS, and Greg Dale, PhD

Make the Big Time Where You Are! by Frosty Westering

Coaching and Control by William Warren

Coaching and Winning by William Warren

Suggested Websites

coachmeyer.com

The official Don Meyer website. Coach Meyer is the all-time winningest NCAA men's basketball coach and a master teacher of the intangibles of the game. Bookmark this site. It has something for everyone—coaches, players, parents, and fans of the game.

kcsbasketball.com

The author's website including a blog, a signup for *Coach Sivils' Roundball Report*, a regular e-newsletter, a page for downloads of a wide range of coaching information, and other interesting things for basketball coaches.

coachsilver.com

Coach Duane Silver's website. Coach Silver has an outstanding e-newsletter every coach should sign up for. He has a vast knowledge of the game of basketball and know some of the best basketball minds in the United States. His newsletter always offers something inspirational or informative.

roundball.net

Coach Doug Porter's website. Porter is one of the most innovative offensive coaches in the nation, and his Lady Tigers at Olivet Nazarene University are always among the highest-scoring teams in the nation.

mensbasketballhoopscoop.blogspot.com

This site is fascinating for coaches who are clinic and X and O junkies. Coach Peterman's site is dedicated to reviewing new coaching books and DVDs and lets coaches swap clinic notes. Be careful if you go to this site—you could spend hours looking at all of the information, which is all up to date.

hoopthoughts.blogspot.com

Coach Bob Starkey maintains this outstanding site. The information on it ranges from reviews of coaching books and DVDs to clinic announcements, Xs and Os, motivational items, and a wide range of interesting items for basketball coaches. One of my favorite sites.

winninghoops.com

The site of the award-winning basketball coaching magazine *Winning Hoops* by Lessiter Publications. This site has a range of interesting items including blogs by well-known coaches.

Chapter Sixteen

Thoughts on Winning

"The most important thing in the game of basketball is the concept of TEAM!"
—Mike Roller

"Losers have tons of variety. Champions take pride in just learning to hit the same old boring winners."
—Vic Braden

"The successful man has enthusiasm. Good work is never done in cold blood, heat is needed to forge anything."
—Harry S. Truman

"I don't like losing much. Winning is much more fun."
—Bill Reidy

"Nothing can stop the man with the right mental attitude from achieving his goal; nothing on earth can help the man with the wrong mental attitude."
—Thomas Jefferson

"There are two kinds of people in this world, givers and takers. We want givers on this team. Takers may get everything they

want, but they won't get the thing they want most: happiness. Givers might not win the game, but they will find happiness in the act of competing and being a good teammate and in the process will do what is right in God's eyes."
—Jack Trager

"It is always better to focus on the process and not the outcome. If you control the process, you will have more control of the outcome. Focusing on the process allows you to be in the moment. Being in the moment allows you to enjoy the act of competing. By focusing on the process, you are controlling the only things you have control over in the game: your attitude, effort, and the choices you make. This allows you to enjoy the experience even if you do not win the game. Focusing on the process also makes it more likely you will win the game as well."
—Kevin Sivils

"The cause of every individual and team slump is the failure to properly perform basic
fundamentals."
—Don Meyer

"Winning is a byproduct of doing things right."
—Don Meyer

"After a loss real competitors want to know when they play again. Losers just want to know when do they eat."
—Paul Westhead

"The will to win is overrated. Everyone wants to win. What matters is the will to prepare to win."
—Bob Knight

"Times such as ours have always bred defeatism. But there remains, nonetheless, some few among us who believe man has within him the capacity to meet and overcome even the greatest challenges of the time. If we want to avoid defeat, we must wish to know the truth and be courageous enough to act upon it. If we get to know the truth and
    have courage, we need not despair."
—Albert Einstein

"Complacency: in warfare more planes are lost coming back after a successful mission than during battle because the crew relaxes."
—Unknown

"Use your best players, not your worst... It sounds simple but a lot of coaches get away from this."
—Don Meyer

"Habits are critical for players... They can't think and play well."
—Don Meyer

"An important part of coaching is to eliminate excuses by players."
—Don Meyer

"If you want to win a national championship, run a single post offense."
—Adolph Rupp

"You are a poor specimen if you can't handle the pressure of adversity."
—Don Meyer

"Every player wants to be taught if he (she) really wants to be a player."
—Don Meyer

"If you are going to bite butts with a bear, don't let the bear have the first bite."
   —Bob Hamilton

"Learn to handle winning, because success can destroy you easier than failure."
   —Don Meyer

"I am only sure about three things in basketball: you have to be a TEAM or nothing else matters, you have to have your players in good stances on offense and defense, and you have to play VERY HARD!"
—Kevin Sivils

"Players have to understand they must serve one another to succeed."
—Dick Bennett

"Less is more; if you add something, you have to take something away."
—Dick Bennett

"Do not confuse simple with easy."
—Rick Anderson

"Focus on two or three things, be consistent. Focus on thirty or forty things and you will see no improvement."
—Rick Anderson

"In Russia if you get bored as an athlete, you go to Siberia. Strive to perfect a few things and really go with those things. The basics are the key!"
—Rick Anderson

"Winning is a byproduct. Good things take time, and they should."
—John Wooden

"Play against the game, not your opponent."
—Bud Wilkinson

"The best players have the best work habits."
—Woody Hunt

"Coaching is preparation."
—Pete Carril

"The most important thing is team morale."
—Dean Smith

"Duty is the most beautiful word in the English language."
   —Robert E. Lee

"Expect greatness and nothing else."
   —George Patton

"Teams struggle with the disease of 'me.'"
   —Pat Riley

"The way to improve the team is to improve ourselves."
   —John Wooden

"Do what you are supposed to and success will follow."
—John Wooden

"It is what you learn after you know it all that counts."
—John Wooden

"We can't control everything that happens to us but we can control the way we face up to it."
—Darrell Royal

"You aren't a loser until you quit trying."
—Mike Ditka

"There are no traffic jams along the extra mile."
—Roger Staubach

"It is more important to hold the players' confidence than their affection."
—Vince Lombardi

"They said you have to use your five best players but I found you win with the five who fit together best."
—Red Auerbach

"You can't measure success until you have failed."
—Steffi Graf

"It all starts at the top."
—Morgan Wooten

"Be sure your team knows they can win and knows how they will win the game. They must understand what it takes."
—Don Meyer

"Don't complicate winning."
  —Bob Knight

"It is not what you teach, it is what you emphasize."
—Pat Head

About the author

A twenty-four-year veteran of the coaching profession, with twenty-two of those years spent as a varsity head coach, Kevin Sivils amassed 464 wins, and his teams earned berths in the state playoffs in nineteen out of twenty-two seasons, advancing to the state semifinals three times. An eight-time coach of the year award winner, Coach Sivils has traveled as far as the Central African Republic to conduct coaching clinics. His first stint was as an assistant coach for his alma mater, Greenville College in Illinois.

Coach Sivils holds a BA from Greenville College with a major in physical education and a minor in social studies, and an MS in kinesiology with a specialization in sport psychology from Louisiana State University. He also has a sport management certification from the United States Sports Academy.

In addition to being a basketball coach, Sivils is a classroom instructor and has taught US government, US history, the history of World War II, and physical education. He has served as an athletic director and assistant athletic director and has been involved in numerous professional athletic organizations.

Sivils has published fourteen previous books, including *Game Strategy and Tactics for Basketball: Bench Coaching for Success*, published by Dog Ear Publishing.

Sivils is married to the former Lisa Green of Jackson, Michigan. They are the proud parents of three children: Danny,

Katie, and Emily. Rounding out the Sivils family are three dogs: Angel, Berkeley, and Al. A native of Louisiana, Coach Sivils currently resides in the great state of Texas.

Also by Kevin Sivils

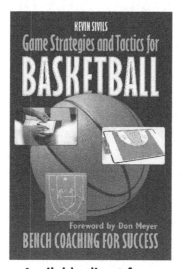

Available direct from

KCS Basketball Enterprises

at www.kcsbasketball.com.

**Also available from Amazon.com
and at Sysko's Sports.**

What others are saying about *Game Strategy and Tactics for Basketball: Bench Coaching for Success:*

"*Game Strategy and Tactics for Basketball* is a great compilation of ideas and thoughts that any coach of any sport at any level can benefit from. I have been involved in coaching basketball

at the collegiate and scholastic levels for twenty-five years and gained great insight and ideas from reading this book. As a coach you can never stop learning, regardless of how long you have been in the profession. I have known Coach Sivils since 2002, and he is one of the most knowledgeable coaches I have ever known. He willingly shares his thoughts in this book. His thought-provoking approach makes for an easy read that will definitely stimulate thought and, most likely, change the way you go about coaching!"
—Rusty Rogers, two-time NAIA Division II Women's National Championship coach and two-time NAIA National Coach of the Year

"Coach Kevin Sivils is a respected coach and administrator who knows what is important in the game of basketball from actual game and practice experience. Split-second decisions from the bench are often the defining moments in highly competitive games at any level. The ability to instantly and accurately give your team its best chance to win under pressure with a reasoned and wise gut decision cannot be underestimated. Your first step should be to read Kevin's book and then put his principles to use in your coaching career as you plan your strategy and tactics for the season and individual games."
—Jack Bennett, head coach (retired), University of Wisconsin-Stevens Point, NCAA Men's Division III National Champions 2004 and 2005

"Coach Sivils's book is the best I have ever read on the topic of bench coaching. I wish I'd had this information all in one place twenty years ago, because Coach Sivils addresses EVERY aspect of getting your team ready to win those close games: time and score situations, selecting the right defensive or offensive strategy, making substitutions, and maximizing

your home-court advantage. If you have been looking for a rigorously thorough handbook on basketball tactics and strategy, you have found it!"
—**Doug Porter, head women's coach, Olivet Nazarene University national scoring leaders 2005, 2006, 2007, 2008; Chicagoland Collegiate Athletic Conference Champions 2000, 2005, 2007**

"Coach Sivils clearly brings his experience in the game of basketball to his writing. He is a great teacher who acquired great gifts over the years, and it's great he wants to share those gifts with other coaches."
—**Bill Reidy, longtime, successful high school and AAU coach**

"Coach Sivils's book has a perfect combination of philosophical viewpoints and in-game Xs and Os strategy. A great example of this approach to organizing the information in this book is the section discussing the importance of controlling what you can control, and another that contains approaches to time and score situations. This is a great book for a young or veteran coach!"
—**Robbie White, former player of Coach Sivils, and first-year varsity head coach**

To order additional copies of this book in team quantities, contact Coach Sivils by e-mail at info@kcsbasketball.com. Special pricing is available for team orders.

www.kcsbasketball.com

Made in the USA
Middletown, DE
08 April 2019